PRAISE FOR THE "KEEP IT SIMPLE" BOOK

"In a complex world, Simon's techniques for simplicity and cutting through to what really matters always make decision taking so much easier and results so much better. He is astute, perceptive and his brilliant toolkit works – small changes add up to a massive overall improvement."
Alison Straszewski, Deputy Treasurer, TSB Bank plc

"Over the years I have been working with Simon, his insights, rules of thumb and often interesting and quirky exercises have helped immensely! Tools to help me put my thoughts in order and challenges in perspective, and to think through how my actions will affect the business. Most of all Simon has helped me identify and be true to what really matters, and through this book, many others will have access to some of that help."
Terry Watts, International Business Director, Activate Learning

"Where there is a challenge Simon is able to get to the heart of it quick, slicing away distractions and noise. His ability to do so reminds me of samurai warrior. Clean, quick and simple."
Kim Ann Curtin, Founder and CEO, The Wall Street Coach

"Simon cuts to the chase and our conversations have left me with greater belief in my thinking, my methods and my management style. His methodologies present simple solutions for complicated people. His Simple Notes are thought-provoking, sometimes challenging, often off-the-wall and always a pleasure to read and digest."
Ted Roger, Managing Director, FPP

"Simon's approach keeps you moving forward, removes hurdles (including the perceived ones) and holds you true to yourself. In short he 'keeps everything simple' and success follows."
Jennifer Mathias, CFO & Deputy CEO, EFG Private Bank Ltd

*This book is dedicated to
each and every complication
that has shown up in my life
and inspired this work.*

Published by
LID Publishing Ltd
One Adam Street
London
WC2N 6LE
United Kingdom

31 West 34th Street, Suite 8004,
New York, NY 10001, US

info@lidpublishing.com
www.lidpublishing.com

650 · 1

A member of:

Business Publishers Roundtable

www.businesspublishersroundtable.com

© Simon Tyler, 2017
© LID Publishing Ltd, 2017

Printed in the Czech Republic by Finidr

ISBN: 978-1-911498-11-7

Cover and page design: Caroline Li
Illustrations: Sara Taheri

THE "KEEP IT SIMPLE" BOOK

50 WAYS TO UNCOMPLICATE YOUR LIFE AND WORK

SIMON TYLER

LONDON   NEW YORK   BOGOTA
MADRID   BARCELONA   BUENOS AIRES
MEXICO CITY   MONTERREY   SAN FRANCISCO
SHANGHAI

CONTENTS

ACKNOWLEDGEMENTS

Most of the ideas I share here sparked from the experiences and events I have encountered. Where they did not, I have made reference to the source of the thought and I acknowledge those sources later.

I would like to thank many for their role and help, inspiration, ideas, support and challenges to my thinking over the years. My clients have often inadvertently inspired my thought process which has manifested as ideas within these pages. Significant thanks go to Rachelle Mills, Martin Liu and the team at LID, Debbie Pye, Mark Harris, Kate Duffy and David Lambard.

INTRODUCTION:
KEEP IT SIMPLE

Welcome to your personal handbook of strategies to 'Keep It Simple' in your career, work and life.

The impact I seek to cause in the work, careers and lives of my clients is almost always centred on and returns to simplicity. 'Keeping it simple' makes conversations flow, understanding easier, difficulties or blockages get resolved and ideas generated with significantly more ease.

"Keeping it simple" represents the choices I make as I tackle the complexities of my world. It is almost always the most efficient and effective way and it is something you can do too, which I aim to inspire through the *Simple Notes* contained in this book.

Having been gifted the name Simon by my parents, unsurprisingly 'Simple' has been often appended! And so it has become my mantra, my 'go to strategy' when circumstances or assignments get difficult or confusing, when clients get stuck or overwhelmed... simplifying always finds a way forward. I've worked alone, been an employee in big corporations, in small self-start entrepreneurial businesses, within my own companies and have sat on the board of directors of others. As a coach, consultant, facilitator and speaker I have been in some amazing learning situations. It all provides for a plentiful and richly stocked library of case studies.

Over the years I have observed life and business scenarios that are extraordinarily complex. Complications that have festered, grown and led to delays, confusion, disappointment and even commercial paralysis.

There is, always, a simple way, and the mantra 'Keep It Simple' is often spoken, but rarely effectively embedded.

So this is what I've done, and what I do, and how, along the way, I have discovered the things I have. In 2009 I started writing a blog and every few weeks since I have posted whatever was in my thoughts. It could be a client conversation, a challenge I faced at the time, something just read, heard or experienced. And very occasionally it could be something out of proverbial left field, something inexplicable – and these have often been the blogs that received the most feedback and seemingly had the greatest impact with my readers.

I suggest that rather than read this book in a linear way (conventionally from front to back), dip in and take out the thoughts and ideas that are relevant to you on a particular day or week. To help make more sense of the collection, and my other work, I have created a selector tool available on my website (www.simontyler. com). There you will find a *Simple Notes* page with drop-down lists of some of the most common business and personal evolution challenges. Against each I have listed the *simple notes* that offer a way to face the challenge anew.

Throughout this book I pose questions that you may be tempted to only briefly consider and superficially answer. For full effect I urge you to stop and think through your response to the question. Perhaps even pick up a pen and get the thoughts down on paper.

Once you have consumed a few of the notes, you will begin to notice some foundational themes regarding making positive personal change. My core coaching beliefs and my *Simple Notes* tend to be based on:

You get what you think about, whether you want it or not.

Thoughts trigger feelings; feelings trigger actions, which in turn create the results in your world (every time).

When you understand where your thoughts come from and what triggers them, then you are a long way down the evolutionary road.

And I always come back to the importance of simplicity:

When life is tough, simplifying makes things better.

When life is great, simplifying makes things better.

My hope is that you keep this book with you, or close to hand, and go to it as you need, whether it be for a recharge or an idea or a way through or perhaps a topic to share with your team. (Feel free to do so; all I ask is that you let them know where the idea came from, and they can subscribe at my site for more.)

I am confident that within these pages you will find many ideas that will resonate and surprise you with what is possible. As you begin to experience success and positive change do please do let me know, as your reportable results will inspire others.

To 'Keep It Simple' is your choice. It's a choice that you can make whenever you want or need.

Simon Tyler, October 2016
www.simontyler.com

HOW TO USE
THIS HANDBOOK

This book is designed to be short and easily digestible.

Each of the *Simple Notes* or chapters stand alone and are ideal to be read in separate instalments. Reading, sharing and acting on one chapter a week will provide personal growth for you wherever you currently find yourself.

The *Simple Notes* have distinct, memorable titles, all headed with an inspiring quote, that in and of itself deserves a moment of reflection.

But as with many books in this field some will naturally resonate with you and others are likely to make you scowl! Let go of any resistance and follow the flow; act on those you like and pass by the rest.

Your options in consuming this book then are:

- Read it linearly and follow each *Simple Note* challenge once a week.

- Read it linearly and mark the pages that resonate with you, acting on them when you are ready.

- Randomly open the book and work with the *Simple Note* from the page you open to.

- Use it as a reference book. Turn to the *Simple Note* that matches the development need of a colleague, a client or your team. Share it with them and work through it together.

As you take more notes into practise you will notice your thinking calming and a more graceful approach to previously challenging situations.

Whatever you choose, enjoy the *Simple Notes*, be challenged and embrace being driven to action. But always, keep it simple.

SIMPLE NOTES...
FOR KEEPING
THINGS SIMPLE

*"I find the great thing in this world is not so much where
we stand, as in what direction we are moving."*

Oliver Wendell Holmes Sr. (1809-1894)

1. AT YOUR BEST?

"Twenty years from now you will be more disappointed by the things you didn't do than by the ones you did do. So throw off the bowlines. Sail away from the safe harbour. Catch the trade winds in your sails. Explore. Dream. Discover."

Mark Twain (1835-1910)

Are you at your best? Right now, today, this week? Are you in a purple patch, in your element, firing on all cylinders?

If not, when were you last at your best? How long did that 'best' moment last and what's changed?

Having observed myself working and, more often, attempting to work, I can absolutely confirm a correlation between being at my best, and results (financial or otherwise), feeling good, efficiency and effectiveness. My ability to influence, to be creative, to inspire others, all happens when I am operating at my best. At all other times some or all of these outcomes elude me.

I've noticed this in almost all of the people with whom I have worked as a coach, over the last 15 years. When they spend moments 'at their best' for a few hours, a day, perhaps even a week or more, amazing things happen. They experience breakthroughs, crystal-clear perspective on topics that were once hazy and performance increases in them and those around them.

So, why would you not want to be at your best all the time?

Well you can be there significantly more often than you might be now.

First, it's a choice – a conscious and determined choice.

You are at the controls of your life and performance; no one else is. You get to decide your reaction to what shows up, you don't have to play the role of victim of the circumstances in which you find yourself. Choose neutral.

Secondly, it's about becoming aware of who you are when you are at your best. What are the circumstances? What has led up to this, and so on, in as much detail as you can identify.

Then, thirdly, it is about creating that context for being your best every day.

Here's a suggestion, coined by my masterful coaching friend Kate Duffy. Pick up your pen and write uninterrupted for at least three minutes, completing the following sentence:

'I'm at my best when...'

Revisit this often, then notice what the recurring ingredients are. These conditions could be actively put in place – particularly on days when your world is demanding more of you than you feel you have available! Work on them, adding, subtracting, adapting them one at a time, and you will be creating the circumstance where being your best becomes easier and your best will just get better!

2. NOISE

*"Always bear in mind that your own resolution to succeed
is more important than any other one thing."*

Abraham Lincoln (1809-1865)

There is so much noise around us. Traffic, conversations, music, the
buzz of a PC, the ping of incoming emails, texts, notifications, even
the hum of overhead lights. What about the most challenging noise
of all – that inner voice, the half-thoughts, the emotional outbursts
and second thoughts? What a cacophony of white noise!

The ability to concentrate on more than one conscious thought
is more of a challenge today than ever before. I have noticed attention spans (the purest, most alert, creative and aware type of
attention) in professional business people being reduced to just a
few minutes, as they drift in and out of clarity. It may seem like your
attention stays on task for the hour or two set aside, but in truth,

this is not the case. Distractions knock your focus often, demanding that you zero in again and again. Your way of working simply isn't working!

Yes, business life is fast-paced, decisions need to be made, information assimilated, messages delivered, people influenced. Today's leaders are feeling the strain – often a decision is not quite right, information is missed, messages are poorly thought through, they're poorly communicated and influence is diminished.

Now could be the time to work on this, and reactivate the skills and creativity that reside in the quieter parts of your mind.

There are many techniques I have found, been taught and experimented with, and as I discover more they will be reported on my blog (www.simontyler.com). Your thinking needs more space: room to allow new thoughts and ideas to form, and space to listen, to watch and notice what's going on around you. And I'm not necessarily talking about hours here; you can start this process of change with just a few moments every day. Here are a few starters:

Write – In Julia Cameron's book *The Artist's Way* she suggests starting each day by writing three pages (just write – don't judge it, don't even read it, just write). The act of writing helps unblock thoughts, to expressiveness. In effect, to warm up your mind for the day ahead.

Pause – Count to three (to yourself, not out loud) before answering a question or contributing a comment. This is surprisingly sufficient time for your brain to consider a mass of information. Your subsequent comment shifts from 'reaction' to a more considered 'response'.

Breathe – Twice a day take a moment to actively breathe in, hold and slowly breathe out. Repeat 10 times and notice how your state will change, away from anxious, tense, angry, stressed or concerned, to being calmer, clearer and more open.

Talk – Dialogue with a coach, mentor or trusted colleague is a great way to unravel entangled thoughts, to hear yourself express and create a quiet space – just for you – in an otherwise noisy day.

Choose one, work with it for a week and find your preferred 'noise filter'.

3. INTERRUPT YOUR SLUMP

*"One of the secrets of success is to refuse
to let temporary setbacks defeat us."*

Mary Kay (1918-2001)

We are all emotionally connected, to some degree, to the people and events around us. These outside influences often trigger what seems to be an automated emotional reaction and from there thoughts, feelings and moods blossom or fade. Are these always the most empowering and useful choices, which is what they un-consciously become? Probably not.

Chances are that your reaction may actually be reducing your power, restricting your creative subconscious and placing you in a weakened state. Your ability to respond appropriately – to decide, to think in straight lines, to engage your full intuitive self – becomes restricted.

In the midst of the reaction process is a physical shift, which triggers your emotional response. It could be a shrug, a frown or even some kind of deflated slump. There are many 'slump reactions': shoulders dropping, head shifting down and chin forward, an exaggerated exhale (or huff!) with a curved back, and many more subtle varieties...all of them notably slump-worthy.

It's likely that you have unknowingly refined and engrained your slump reaction style over the years, and with it comes a pre-arranged set of thoughts, feelings and moods that your brain has linked to the slump. No matter how subtle or even undetectable they may be to others, your slump reaction is currently setting you up for a pattern of being 'less than your best'.

As I watched a Test Match I noticed members of the England cricket team slump when their match-winning batting star was out early. Unsurprisingly (to me), the subsequent batsmen struggled to get their 'heads back into the game'. It's an expression widely used in sport and just as applicable in business.

At a business meeting, I noticed slump reactions to a particular corporate message regarding cost-cutting and potential reorganization. The subsequent conversations on a completely different topic were less creative or positively solution-oriented than they could have been.

I challenge you for the next couple of weeks to discover your slump reaction and notice when it happens. Laugh when you catch it happening, interrupt it and choose an alternative. Try a more powerful upright stance, and take in a few active breaths. Your brain may still throw up some habitual reactions to the situation, but you will see it more clearly for what it is, and actually have, and discover, a range of more appropriate responses at your disposal.

After a week of slump-interruptions you will start to notice a change in your moods and capabilities in situations that previously would have annoyed, frustrated, flummoxed or even floored you.

4. SET-UP

"We cannot solve our problems from the same level of thinking that created them."

Albert Einstein (1879-1955)

How are you set up? For success, for failure, for whatever shows up? Are you positioned for a good time or not? I'm not referring to how you are innately wired, but more how you 'set yourself up' to perform.

What is your set-up? Are you even aware of this? Do outside forces affect your set-up from day to day? And if they do, is that all the time, or as a consequence of random external circumstances?

In my coaching I have noticed that a person's set-up very accurately and literally sets up his or her experience and results every day. If you tell yourself today is going to be frantic, stressful or a struggle, it probably will be.

You will have a few 'set-ups' that you frequently engage, albeit unconsciously. Let's take the frantic set-up. Your brain recognizes and responds to the set-up brilliantly. It focuses your attention exclusively on any evidence of 'frantic'. It seeks it out, defocuses everything else and shines a metaphorical light on the proof. It holds your muscles and body shape in a rehearsed tensed fashion ready to 'franticize'.

In this state it becomes difficult to think your way out of frantic, to problem solve, to be serene and sometimes even to calm down at all. The probability is that even if the situations you find yourself in aren't actually frantic, somehow you'll make them so or magnetically find something or someone to exercise your adrenaline-charged set-up.

This is the same for all your set-ups, whether you are aware of them or not. Whatever your set-up, you will attract situations, people and incidences that match your mindset – what power you have!

I challenge you to become aware of your set-ups. There are often times in the day when you shift a set-up, and therefore get to upgrade it, if you exercise awareness and your freedom to choose. The common set-up moments are first thing in a morning, break times, formal meetings and work-to-home transition times.

Step into your set-up process and choose your own setting. While external factors can affect your day, it is your 'set-up' that gives them the impact they need. When you deliberately select your set-up you become resistant to slipping into old set-up habits and soon bring supportive events, people and situations to bed in your chosen setting.

5. WORDS

"Be not careless in deeds, nor confused in words,
nor rambling in thought."

Marcus Aurelius (121-180)

"Have something to say, and say it as clearly as you can. That is
the only secret of style."

Matthew Arnold (1822-1888)

I once heard the expression that language for humans is both the greatest gift and the greatest curse. In my coaching and facilitation work, I have experienced both sides of this.

The words you choose (sometimes unconsciously, out of habit) reflect your current thinking, but also significantly affect your future thinking, not to mention others who may be in earshot.

Brain science has proved that, in a predictable way, your thoughts impact how you feel, which directly impacts the actions you take and the results you get, or indeed the next situation you find yourself in.

Once those thoughts are voiced out loud the impact is doubled. But, critically, the person most influenced by your words is YOU!

What do you repeatedly say?

How do you habitually describe things?

I recently described a situation as tense, overwhelming, snowed-under, messy and disorganized. And before I knew it, my *thinking* matched this perfectly. Almost immediately, I didn't *feel* good, and crucially I couldn't 'think' my way out of it.

I shifted my words, not being delusional or false in my revised internal dialogue, just ensuring they were better chosen. I reminded myself of my abilities to work through situations, of the resources I always seem to find. And slowly my thought patterns altered. Feelings of being overwhelmed faded, allowing me to upgrade the words I used still further, and the difficult situation that was, wasn't!

Notice your words. Do they describe the situation you want to be in, stay in or move to? Or are they painting you further in to a situation you want to avoid? You get to choose, and don't forget who's listening.

Bonus simple note: Word Up!

If you find yourself drifting back to the old language, experiment with these super-fixes to upgrade your words.

Choose one to trial, starting today, or work through them all, if you're up for it and are ready to word-up. They will have an impact on your brain's word production.

Today – For the next 24 hours, do not complain to anyone. About anything. If you catch yourself complaining before the 24 hours are up, simply begin again. When I first took this challenge it took me nine days to complete, since then, however, I have almost eliminated my propensity to complain and now take responsibility for everything in which I am involved (not least my reaction to it). Each time I retake this challenge, I get closer to a straight complaint-free 24-hours.

This Week – For the next week, do not gossip or entertain gossip about anyone, from anyone. If someone persists in attempting to gossip with you, you may ask them to stop, explain this exercise, or simply walk away. If you catch yourself gossiping before the week is up, simply begin again. Talking about people is purported to be the lowest grade of energy in a dialogue, and often leaves both talker and listener in one way or another drained, which is further evidence of the need to word-up.

This Month – For the next month, do not criticize any member of your family, inner circle of friends or your team. You may of course make requests of them if there is something you would like them to do differently. Be honest with yourself as to whether or not your request is a genuine appeal or a secret criticism. If you catch yourself criticizing a team member, close friend or family member before the end of the month, simply begin again.

Each of these experiments targets the root of your thinking, and capacity for word production, and can support a permanent change in both.

To embed this note a little further, before taking action yourself, observe colleagues for a few days, focusing on the language they repeatedly use to describe their world and their challenges. What preconceived notions and mindsets emerge, and what do they reveal about them?

6. WHEN?

"Yesterday is gone. Tomorrow has not yet come.
We only have today. Let us begin."

Mother Teresa (1910-1997)

In her coaching business, Kate Duffy often uses the phrase 'If not now, when?' What a great challenge to most of us, most of the time, to simply begin!

Are you putting up with stuff and waiting for the (undefined) perfect moment or set of circumstances, resources, or ideas to solve or change it? Do you have intentions that simply aren't acted on, because they are not urgent, sitting in the background, waiting until the 'ideal' time?

Your work or personal life is being held back in some way, your happiness, enjoyment, your full throttle effort, until... when? In short, have you suspended the full you, until your 'when' happens?

'When' is a cute little word. It can trick you into putting up with your current situation, on the basis that it will, at some point, in a non-defined future, be resolved. It goes into your mental 'pending' tray, ready to remind and irritate you, every day, occupying space and never shifting. It becomes an invisible excuse preventing you from taking inspired action in the direction of your goals, whatever they may be.

Kate's challenge – 'If not now, when?' – can be levelled at all of the areas in which you are stalling. It doesn't necessarily mean you take action on all of them now. It simply invites you to examine the blockage, and check whether it is important enough to take action on now. Or, does it even need to be there at all – you might give yourself permission to simply let it go. If it's not ready for release or new action, then diminish its importance and allow it to be parked, and don't mention it again until the next review.

From time to time I catch myself in situations when I can palpably feel clouds of gloom gathering around me. Mostly I am aware of this and take action early to shift my thinking.

Set yourself a series of questions that help you think through your position. Don't just think the answers; write them down, or get someone to ask you the questions for you to answer out loud:

- *What doesn't feel good, or right?*

- *What am I putting up with, or what is it that seems to be dragging, difficult or problematic right now?*

- *What am I waiting for?*

- *Even if the above factors are true, what steps can I take today to shift direction?*

- *What would it feel like to know that 'when' has become 'now'?*

Good luck; go ahead and make your change. If not now, when?

7. REBOOT

"Finish each day and be done with it. You have done what you could. Some blunders and absurdities no doubt crept in; forget them as soon as you can. Tomorrow is a new day. Begin it well and serenely and with too high a spirit to be cumbered with your old nonsense."

Ralph Waldo Emerson (1803-1882)

Most of us are mentally working on or processing everything that remains outstanding in our work and personal life, all day long. The more there is, the more energy it is taking up, rendering you less powerful and resourceful and leaving you feeling drained.

Every piece of paper, unopened email, lingering task and unfinished conversation is using up your human RAM depleting your brain's storage capacity. When you reach your own 'full' point, many things change.

Your mental and physical state changes and you are more likely to react to the day's events rashly, disproportionately, become irritable or just feel overwhelmed most of the time, never sure exactly what it is that is causing the fug. You may become physically tired, and the emotional changes can make you feel like anything you do makes little difference to your virtual to-do list – that you are simply not getting anywhere.

When you take action to complete a task, you regain a more powerful state, are able to gain mental clarity over what's going on and experience overview rather than overwhelm. The action you take isn't necessarily completing all the tasks; the whole point is that life is so busy nowadays it isn't about ticking every single item off your list. Rather, it's about shifting your attitude and taking inspired action instead of frantic scattergun action.

The technique you should consider here is rather like clicking 'Control-Alt-Delete', (which is its own Simple Note, #44) on a PC to see what processes are running in the background. There are often unnecessary programmes running that you can instantly close, and a few that you can simply switch off too. The same applies to all the things running through your mind. Look at them, review your thoughts and shift your attitude toward them. This reboot can move you to a significantly more resourceful place. And from there you can begin again.

I recommended that you take a major personal reboot from time-to-time, at least once each year. This is my quick five-stage reboot:

Thought Unload – Sit silently for a few minutes and allow the spray of thoughts to pour out onto paper. Write down everything you think may be in there. You may or may not take action on some of them; simply unloading them to paper can be liberating.

Work Area Cleanse – Desks get cluttered, with urgent, non-urgent, important and unimportant stuff. Be ruthless and march through the paperwork inbox, making instant decisions about every item: bin it, file it, do tomorrow or do this week (no more deliberating!).

Email Purge – In busy phases many emails build up and require diary decisions, commitments or comment. Spend some more ruthless time cleaning up this volume. Work quickly; in doing so you are activating your (often over indulged) intuitive decision-making frequency. Tune in and act.

Waiting for Me – Who is waiting for you, expecting something from you or owed something by you? Over the next seven days complete as many of these as you can. This includes delivering words of thanks, appreciation and gratitude that remain outstanding – some of these may go back a while and can be profoundly liberating once completed.

Waiting for You – Who are you waiting for, who owes you, from whom are you wishing or wanting a word of thanks or gratitude? In truth you cannot control their completion, but you can instantly modify your attitude toward the incompletes and cease the draining effect of each. Let go of the expectations and clear them out. If any nice words from others materialize, that's a bonus.

Enjoy stepping up into your powerful and resourceful state each time you reboot.

8. CONQUERING THE EMAIL DRAGON

*"Man must cease attributing his problems to his environment,
and learn to exercise his will – his personal responsibility..."*

Albert Schweitzer (1875-1965)

Email overload is rife. As more devices and forms of communication are added to our lives, the time we devote to emails diminish-
es further. Yet, the mental and physical impact of an out-of-control
email inbox persists.

Your relationship with your email inbox can make a significant difference in your work rates, your stress levels and your overall communication efficiency.

Here are some suggestions to conquer your roaring email dragon. I don't necessarily recommend them, only recommend that you consider them. Your world may have codes of conduct that mean some of these are too hasty, reckless or simply inappropriate. Just consider the suggestions that could be a simple step for you.

The following 10 measures go beyond obvious, common-sense moves like switching off auto-notifiers, asking people you know to reduce email, use of a junk mail filter, shortening your email content, etc. Let's assume you've already taken those steps.

1.   Stop using 'Reply All'. Unless everyone truly needs to read your reply, keep it simple and answer the sender only. Be ready to apologize to those who feel left out of some email loops – explain why you're doing it.

2.   Be more specific in the subject line. Even if recipients never get to open your email or delete it on sight, they will always view the subject line. Be clearer, punchier and more specific. Tell them what you want to do with the content. Consider including the acronym 'EOM' in the title bar to inform the reader that the title bar is in fact the 'End of Message!'

3.   Deal with mail as it arrives. Respond to it, act on it, read it, whatever. If you haven't dealt with it or even opened it in seven days, delete it.

4.   Process email at set times only. A high volume of email has an incredible nudging power that grabs your attention. Where you place your attention remains your immense potential power, so don't give it away lightly.

5.   Find out about software that filters mail by type – there will be several types in your company, in your network or available on the web to test and incorporate.

6.   Clear your inbox every day – action them, file them, put them in your new 'seven-day waiting' folder or delete them.

7.   Set up different email addresses – keep private email separate from work and perhaps set up more than one work address (e.g. one for customers, one for your team and one for everything else).

8.   Send fewer emails – think about what you want to cause, provoke, change, influence. Email is the go-to habit in many companies and not necessarily the most effective option.

9.   Don't reply to every message for example (with 'thanks' or 'will do') – people are aware of their colleagues' email volume and rarely expect, or even want, the politeness of such a response. If you think it rude, clear it up in person.

10. Unsubscribe from lists that you have not read for more than 3 months. Stop accumulating unopened mail; you're storing it somewhere in your head as well as in the inbox. These notes served their time and will come back into focus again when you need them.

And if the dragon is still roaring:

11. Delete All. Extreme action in extreme cases, evaluate the risk and do it. The important stuff comes around again.

Don't forget to let those in your team and extended network know what you are doing and don't be surprised if your email drag-on-slaying strategy seems odd to them.

Social media (Twitter, Facebook, LinkedIn, Flickr, Instagram, Snap-Chat, WhatsApp, etc.) are transforming the way we communicate. Email will gradually move down the communication preference list and join snail-mail letters and paper memos as the 'old way' in which we communicated. So even if you do nothing with your current Email Dragon, its flames will soon no longer burn so brightly.

With that decline needs to go your mental association with email as well.

9. YOUR VERY OWN CIA

"If you want the rainbow, you gotta put up with the rain."

Jimmy Durante (1893-1980)

Do you change your attitude and maybe even your behaviour when things aren't going to plan? How about when decisions are made that directly affect you and limit your immediate choices? Or even when a set of unexpected and annoying circumstances show up?

In these moments a whole set of reactions fire off that alter the way you act for the next few minutes, hours, or, if it's really bad, days. And, unsurprisingly, once you get into that unwanted state you seem to attract more of it!

Clearly, this is not taking you to your best, most productive and most powerful state. Instead, it is sapping any enjoyment you could have. It's just not a good place to be.

It sounds too simplistic when the advice you may frequently receive is 'you have a choice here'. But you really do, and here's a simple thinking process to help.

For a long time I have worked with my clients on 'acceptance' which is the opposite of 'resistance'. The latter causes friction and 'dis-ease', the former is a free-flowing state in which you maintain access to your full thinking and action-taking capability.

'R'evolutionary' coach Seán Weafer coined a great acronym to help here: 'CIA'. CIA is a question process to take you out of moaning, resisting and gritting teeth through to a more powerful non-resisting place of acceptance.

Control – Can I control this situation? If I can, in any way, then let's take action and do it. If not, move on...

Influence – Can I influence anything around this situation? Can I speak to anyone, send information, and change its impact in some way? If I can, in any way, then let's get into action and do it. If not, move on...

Accept it, for now – This doesn't mean give in; it is an in-the-moment invitation to accept whatever it is... for now. From here I can choose to get on with something else, relax into the aftermath, see it for what it is and so on.

I implement my CIA often, as soon as I begin to feel ratty about a situation or meeting or interaction. I regularly experience a significant reduction in the amount of time I feel physically tense, which is a healthier and more productive way to be, and certainly uses less energy, preventing me from becoming drained and no fun to be with.

Good luck with calling in your CIA this week. Run through the questions often. It can help if you work through this with a colleague. Have them ask the questions and hold you to your answers. Regain your power and avoid letting situations turn you into a grouch!

10. SPRINT

"After one has discovered what is he is called for, he should set out to do it with all of the power that he has in his system."
Martin Luther King Jr., (1929-1968)

People circle around ever-growing to-do lists. This can lead them to a feeling of being off the pace, falling behind, under-achieving and missing out on the important actions at the cost of the urgent.

This inadvertent delaying tactic can be linked to some bigger, un-spoken – and therefore unanswered – questions about purpose, direction and meaning of all those itty-bitty tasks. In order to get to that, a crucial first step is to recreate some momentum.

Some time ago I was inspired with a Julius Caesar story. Putting aside some of his methods and political ambitions, it is difficult not to be amazed at the amount Caesar achieved. During his lifetime he became renowned for his *celeritas*, a Latin word meaning 'speed' or 'quickness'. Time and time again he would act so quickly that his opponents were caught completely unawares.

The flip side of this was that he would sometimes act impulsively or rashly and get himself into difficulties as a result. But no one was better than he at getting himself out of difficulties again – again by his innate speed and effectiveness.

You can use this principle of *celeritas* in your own life. To do so, for certain periods of time practise working and moving a little bit faster than you usually do.

This is remarkably effective because, if you move faster than normal, you don't give yourself time to procrastinate, you don't think 'I'll do that later' or 'I really don't want to do that'. You just do it.

Initially try it for a short period. Thirty minutes seems to be my optimum *celeritas* time. Set a timer and just go all out to do as much that you can in that time. Don't spend any time thinking what to do next, just get on with whatever comes to hand. Sending (or deleting) emails, clearing desk space, emptying the dishwasher, responding to meeting requests, just get them done! Irrespective of their scale, their urgency or their apparent relevance.

You may be surprised at how much you achieve. And you may also be very surprised to find that instead of being tiring, it is extremely energising to act in this way. Once momentum begins, the bigger picture almost always comes more clearly into view.

Build up your momentum – creating productivity muscles with *celeritas*.

11. PAUSE

"The right word may be effective, but no word was ever as effective as a rightly timed pause."

Mark Twain (1835-1910)

In contrast to the earlier *Simple Note* on the power of an all-out sprint, this note discusses the opposite.

Pause.

Like many, you may be experiencing an increase in the demands on your time and a demand for speedier decision-making, while facing an increase in distractions, options and alternatives. Put simply, there's a lot going on, for everyone. We have created situations that call for us to be alert and switched-on all day long.

Your default strategy becomes 'press on through', getting whatever needs to be done, done. Some important stuff gets put off, – perhaps needing *celeritas* time to get them done; refer back to *Simple Note* 10 – and your attitude and activity becomes tensely charged, frantic, even erratic. This can develop into that unwanted state of being overwhelmed and, in extreme cases, spiral into pointlessness.

How many of these apply to you?

● Clutter has increased in and around your workplace.

● You are double-tasking (emailing while on conference calls, texting while watching TV, etc.).

● You take several 'gap' tasks with you everywhere (even to the rest room).

● In any lull you turn to your phone, tablet or laptop screen to check for new emails or notifications.

● You get bored early in meetings and conversations, wanting to cut to the chase without any preamble or irrelevant dialogue.

● You catch yourself tidying up other people's workplaces (or similar tasks that have nothing to do with your to-do list).

● You are re-reading difficult or complex emails without taking any action (the information just doesn't seem to register on the first pass).

- You miss or compromise meal times.

- Your concentration on tasks is reduced (it hurts to hold focus).

- You fill silent moments with radio, music, messaging, making non-urgent calls (silence and nothing-time feels uncomfortable).

- You are extremely irritable when trapped in circumstances out of your control (for example, when you are stuck in traffic, particularly in an area with no mobile signal).

- Excess fatigue causes you to fall asleep in front of the television in the evenings.

Each of these, in isolation, is probably excusable and may even be a by-product of you stepping up your productivity at busy times. It is when three or more are combined and occur more frequently or even become a new norm, that change is needed.

Having admitted (to yourself) that some apply to you, consider how they serve you, or not. What is the impact of these behaviours? Are you waiting for something to change before you do? Could now be the time for you to take action?

Indeed, it may be time for you to:

Pause.

Take a moment for the incessant energy to slow down, to give yourself a sense of perspective, to get some height and allow a brief overview of what's going on, to re-engage all mental systems. Just a few minutes – that might be all it takes.

A five-minute pause will be immensely valuable for you. Add another three minutes for each additional item you ticked on the above list. You will find your first pause difficult, as you itch to get back into full-on 'doing' mode. But hold on to your pause moment – the benefits will be worth it.

Try this:

1. Sit quietly in an uninterruptable, clutter-free place. If one doesn't exist, that's the first place to start work: create one.

2. Become aware of tension points around your body (neck, shoulders, face) and allow yourself to switch them off. Say it aloud – verbalize your intent to relax the tensed-up spots – and experience those tense muscles loosening.

3. Breathe deeply and slowly, six to ten times. This will accelerate your ability to relax.

4. As soon you catch yourself going into action-related thoughts, release them, on the agreement (with yourself!) that you will pick them up again in a few moments.

When you're done, press 'play' again.

12. CLEARING SPACE

*"The man who removes a mountain begins
by carrying away small stones."*

Chinese Proverb

The build-up of clutter is a common early indicator that you have lots going on, or you are disorganized – or both. The truth is, it is essentially the same thing.

It has often been said that your workspace is a reflection of your headspace – worryingly true for many. As if to prove it, the opposite can also be true: a clear desk space can make it easier to be more creative and productive. If you dispute that, you're in denial. Not denial that you can be productive in clutter, but denial that you have enormous potential on the other side of your current chaos.

Back in 1983, during Work Experience Week – a European program that offers trial employment opportunities for young people – I was placed at National Panasonic in Slough, a town west of London. Visiting senior management wanted to see desks with one document and one pen on top. They wanted to see nothing other than the studious employee at work with both. Now this may be a touch idealistic, even extreme, in today's workplace, but it remains a great challenge. I would urge you to try the following:

Get everything off your desk that you haven't touched or used in the last 24 hours.

Then try this 33:33:33 purge, which I've found to be helpful every time it has been employed. This can apply to every piece of paper and every email or message:

- 33% – Keep it. This is the important stuff (the original document perhaps). You want to work on it or read it or do something with it soon.

- 33% – Chuck it. This is stuff you've held for too long: old reading material that hasn't been read and won't be. Get rid of it. This includes non-actioned requests that must be past their 'please do this' date.

- 33% – Not sure, and hasn't fallen into either of the previous categories. Box it up and give it to a friend or neighbour on the agreement that, if you don't ask for it back in two weeks, they have permission to dispose of it.

That's two-thirds of the clutter cut in two simple steps.

And, while you're at it, stand still and look again around your work-space. What do you see? Writing this note, here at my desk, I can see a rolled up bit of carpet, a box of printer cartridges, scores of pens and a chair that never gets sat on. Get that sort of clutter out, NOW.

Enjoy your new space.

13. DOUBLE-TASKING

"Do or don't do, there is no try."

Yoda (900 years before the Battle of Endor)

It's a sure sign you've reached the land of the two 'O's (overwhelmed and overcommitted) when your productivity engine has you attempting two or more things at a time. Busy days can see you emailing while on a conference call, attending a meeting while mentally preparing for the next one, working on two documents, messaging and mentally planning your evening, all at the same time.

Brain science has shown that you can only truly be effective at one conscious task (and that goes for men *and* women!). As soon as you mentally split on more than one, while it appears possible, you will block access to subconscious capabilities that could liberate your full potential.

Below your conscious surface you are busy sensing things: the environment you are in, the sounds, sights, feelings, smells and tastes all around you. These brilliant sensory clues sharpen your ability to know what's going on at a given moment. In addition to this, your amazing brain will be accessing files and information to match the sensory data. And, all the while, you will be tuning into your intuitive creative subconscious. Block these channels and you could make mistakes, rendering you *less* effective, not *more* so. You'll miss the nuance in a message, you'll get caught unawares, and your ability to communicate (sensing, listening and talking) will be impaired. Try this three-step plan:

Step One – STOP DOING IT! It's just not worth it, you won't be at your best and the assumed extra productivity will never be never realized.

Step Two – When you catch yourself double-tasking, laugh at yourself. This is a much more empowering starting point than haranguing or damaging self-talk and it gives you a moment to decide which task this moment is calling for. Decide, do it and drop the other task.

Step Three – A double-tasking urge is a call to pause. Take five minutes to follow the *'Pause' Simple Note* and return to the task(s). Have a look at the next two to three hours in your schedule and carve out the time necessary to complete the competing task.

You don't get double-brilliance by double-tasking, more likely half-and-half.

Enjoy the comparative ease and liberation of working on one conscious task, brilliantly. You are incredible at your best, so be in that place as often as you can, handling things one step at a time.

14. BLACKBERRY MOMENTS

"Our doubts are traitors, and make us lose the good we oft might win, by fearing to attempt."

William Shakespeare (1564-1616)

The feeling of being overwhelmed is present or looming nearby when you begin turning every moment into a BlackBerry moment. (Or iPhone, PDA, tablet, mobile phone, etc.)

Today's mobile technology means we are, pretty much, 'always on,' connected with colleagues, customers, friends, information sources, news, data streams... everything is on 24 hours a day.

This is neither a good thing, nor a bad thing. It's just a thing.

When the unspoken story in your head has become "I'm so busy", then unsurprisingly you may develop the habit of turning to your phone or mobile device in every gap, convincing yourself that this is a natural extension of your effectiveness. It is almost laughable that, when I have caught myself in this state, I am refreshing apps and emails on my mobile phone, even though it does it on its own every few minutes. I'm hurrying up new information, rather than appreciating and enjoying a moment of silence!

This will (or already has) become unhelpful for many – you are confusing this constant connection with inspired action. It is not *in*spired; it is expired, in that the motivation for action comes from outside of us. You are not your phone and it is not an extension of you.

I developed *Top 10 Tips for Email Mastery*, within the '*Conquering The Email Dragon*' *Simple Note*. The tips can really support change; in short they include noticing that we are treating every email as urgent, as if they were telephone calls (the audible or visual prompt saying 'answer me, answer me'). Eventually your sense of urgency becomes so overloaded and worn down that you have no time for, and cannot even recognize, the important stuff.

A pause is needed in your proceedings – things are not going to change for you without you being actively involved. This sounds obvious but it's true. Any change will feel uncomfortable – as you shift an ingrained habit, you will feel the strength of the habit pulling you back to your device again and again. Know that this is just the habit playing out, not your choice and not the best thing to do. Be strong.

Here are a few challenges for you to consider:

- Extend the download frequency to four times as long as you have it set now. For me, moving from every 15 minutes to every hour made me super-conscious of the poor habit I was in. I laughed each time I went to my phone ready to download again, stopping just in time, until eventually the new habit was established.

- Leave your phone on its own, away from you, for 24 hours (sounds easy, but I seriously dare you to try it). This is a powerful habit breaker and you will experience curious pangs during the 24-hour freedom period.

- Trial a TLA – 'Technology Liberation Alternator' – an hour fully connected, an hour without, an hour on, an hour off... and be brilliant in each of the phases, making the most of each.

- Become a single taskmaster by switching your device off when you are in a meeting, working on an assignment, writing copy, whatever. Don't just turn the volume down; turn your device off completely. Then turn it on and become that master communicator again.

Find the strength and see it through.

15. RESETTING YOUR DAILY DEFAULT MODE

*"...The last of the human freedoms to choose
one's attitude in any given set of circumstances,
to choose one's own way."*

Viktor Frankl (1905-1997)

Much has been written about the number of thoughts we have every day (something in the order of sixty thousand) and that most of them are broadly the same as the previous day. Accordingly your plans to change and your personal evolution is predictably slow, certainly slower than is possible with a little focused intent.

Some of my personal development work with my coach focused on my thoughts: specifically, shifting from a hands-off way of accepting whatever they might be, to consciously and actively choosing them, and noticing the impact they have on subsequent thoughts and, ultimately, the results I created.

What I discovered in the process – or rather, what I *remembered* in the process – is that the first hours in the day are exponentially more significant when thinking about positive change, developmental and corrective stuff.

Every morning between the time that you wake up and your first appointment you are collecting your thoughts. These regular pattern-thoughts are normally sourced from three places:

- yesterday's events

- today's expected events

- the story you are repeating about your current habitual circumstance ("I never have enough time," "There's too much to do," "I'm rubbish in the morning," etc.).

These stories become your default setting; subsequent thoughts will inevitably become linked to them. It is your mental starting point; thoughts can only move off from here, not necessarily a great place and one that probably requires a lot of effort and a heap of luck to shift upward. Hence, change happens slowly.

What might your recurring story be? Is it the setting that helps you evolve, or keeps you where you are?

The great news is you can change your default. Begin each day with a resetting. Choose a time (same for each day), such as while or just after you brush your teeth. It's important you think about something you believe in, not an outrageous pipe-dream. Make it positive, such as: "I'll use the time I have today brilliantly," "I'll focus my time only on high-importance things today" or "I have resources available to me all day long." Choose, or develop, a statement that feels best to you.

Changing your morning thinking and setting more powerful intentions for the day can mark the distinction between achievers and non-achievers, the evolved and the unevolved, the relaxed and the stressed.

16. TIME AND SPACE

"It doesn't matter how slowly you go, so long as you don't stop."
Confucius (551-479 BC)

Time is a precious commodity. We talk about it constantly. Find time, save time, not enough time, it's time for...etc. One might even say we have become obsessed with it. I have inadvertently used time as a pressure device to get things done (leaving things until the last minute), then changed my physical state because of the lack of it, setting myself up for stress in the belief that time is my only motivator.

Addiction to time manifests itself in a number of ways. When you become addicted, time management training courses will have little or no effect, as it (time) is managing you. Could any of these be you?

The Clock Watcher – Glancing at clocks or your watch, powering up your mobile phone to check the time, not trusting yourself to know the actual time or the elapsed time. This often means you are under constant tension, waiting to move. This is extremely draining!

The Gap Filler – Looking for gaps in your diary and filling them with meetings. Or, worse still, knowing there are unallocated gaps and allowing your current stuff (meetings, checking emails, writing what should be a straight-forward letter) to magically expand to fill them.

The Fast Mover – Not in a smooth, athletic way but in a more frantic, jittery and erratic way (this can be linked to you trying to process too much at once).

The Reduced Attention Spanner – You're double-thinking, wanting to move on to the next thing before fully completing the first task and thus missing the feeling of progress and subtleties in communications and relationships, etc.

The Commitment Avoider – the thought of agreeing to that meeting/ workshop/programme just seems ridiculous. "Where am I going to find the time?" Before you know it, you're missing out on enjoyable, fun or developmental opportunities because you're still caught in the mix of the small, seemingly important (but not really), stuff.

I have coached many executives who find themselves playing out one or more of these roles and I have delivered various time-management training courses over the years. Each of these have confirmed the fact that it's never about time!

While there are deeper things to work on, I have noticed the direct link between TIME and SPACE. I'm not introducing Doctor Who and his TARDIS here. Instead, something much more practical.

The spaces in which you exist have a direct link to the relationship you have with time. Shift one and you will systematically increase the other.

My challenge to you as part of this *Simple Note* is to create space (often the easier of the pair to shift):

● In your schedule – simply create a blank, and fill it with nothing.

● In your workspace – clear your desk; empty a drawer; clear the area around your meeting or other seating areas.

● In your mind – complete tasks (mentally if not physically); sit quietly for 10 minutes (read other *Simple Notes* to evolve your ability to 'pause' brilliantly).

● Find some (physical) space and spend some time there – maybe outdoors, or hold your meeting in a room too big for the participants, perhaps work in a large room on your own. I particularly like this mini-tip as it always delivers a new result; just try it and see. The opposite is also true: small, packed-in meeting rooms are more likely to create tense, clipped conversations, the agenda is more likely to slip and meetings tend to overrun.

● Become aware of the spaces you are in; explore ways to expand the space around you; shift away from confinement.

You will feel the resistance as your ego will still want to panic about the ticking clock as you begin kicking your addiction to time. Keep going. You'll be delighted with what shows up (in the spaces you create!).

17. MOVING ON

"All you have to do is look straight and see the road, and when you see it, don't sit looking at it – walk."

Ayn Rand (1905-1982)

As you make your way through life and encounter tough times and difficult choices, elders may often remind you that 'things are sent to try us'. In many ways they were masterful at enduring these trials, suffering through them for years, even lifetimes. However, remember that rather than just bearing the load, exploring and expanding your potential is your right and your opportunity.

I notice the distinction between people who tolerate stuff and those who do not. There is a pronounced difference in what the latter achieve and how much they seem able to enjoy themselves, be more fully present and more often at their best.

Consider times in your career when you have moved fastest, achieved more, made connections with little effort. Compare that to the times when it's been hard work, you were grinding your teeth in frustration, and what you needed always seemed out of reach.

There is a link between these two states and the amount that you are putting up with. Right now, what are you tolerating or suffering or just plain fed up with?

You have two choices:

1.   Change it.

2.   Change your attitude about it.

Change It – Actually change it; engage in thoughts and conversation about options. Let go of it, step away and release it. You will learn more from letting go than toiling to eventually solve these conundrums. The movement of energy and the vacuum you create will be filled with new people, opportunities and challenges.

If you're not ready for change yet, then your alternate option is to:

Change your attitude toward the problem – Not flippantly, not with a barrage of unconvincing self-talk. No, I mean a real attitude shift. What are the good things about the situation? What are you giving? What are you getting? What are you learning? What more is there to learn? How could this be a powerful experience for you?

There is a third 'choice', and it's the one most people unconsciously make: the 'put up with it' option. However, this is not actually a choice. It doesn't work; you cannot and do not actually 'put' it anywhere. It will almost immediately have a mental, physical and emotional impact on your potential and your power.

Carry too many of these and you may become irritable, find it difficult to relax or to concentrate, begrudge certain tasks or people, and complete them less than brilliantly. Add days or weeks of languishing in this state and you are simply not going to be in a good place.

A great coaching approach that has worked for me is Thomas Leonard's (coachville.com) *Toleration Free Programme*. It is a focused way of zapping the irritators and eliminating elements of our life circumstance that drain you. Sometimes, though, you may find yourself in situations where a bigger decision is required.

When the thing you have been putting up with takes more of your thinking than it should, or irritates or drains you in any way, the choice remains: change it or change your attitude toward it.

"If you don't like something, change it. If you can't change it, change your attitude. Don't complain."

Maya Angelou, poet and civil rights activist

18. BOOST YOUR ENERGY

"Energy and persistence conquer all things."

Benjamin Franklin (1706-1790)

Much of my work with individuals and teams over the last 15 years has involved running behavioural and attitude assessments, helping my clients understand how they, and those around them, are wired. Knowing one's self is simply the best place to begin.

You have a unique make-up and combination of motivators, stressors and natural and learned ways of coping. When the going gets tough and your workload increases, with growing expectations (and less time) you will experience a physical response that you may often ignore, patch over or cope with... but never resolve.

My wish is that you always have the energy you need and that you operate at your best, as much of the time as you can. Your energy, which fuels your attitude, is one of your most powerful tools. If you are deficient in an area in which your make-up thrives you will become drained.

From the following list, establish what delivers relief and re-energizes you. Notice the opposites too and the damage silently sapping your power. You will need your own personal combination of one or more of these activities:

Physical exercise – Even when you feel mentally or emotionally drained and time does not offer the obvious opportunity, exercise could be exactly what's needed to recharge. This could be a run, a competitive game, a swim or simply a brisk walk. Many who need this form of energy-boost often opt for the opposite: vegging out. No energy is gained, fatigue accumulates.

Socialising – Spending time in conversation with friends or colleagues with no agendas, no timetables and no expectations. Those of us who feed on this form of energy boost often opt for the opposite: work harder, alone, and press on... or we throw ourselves into a higher-stress version of socializing with more challenging colleagues or people we don't know. No energy is gained, fatigue is accumulated.

Chill-out time – Engage in stuff with no pressure: TV, reading, music, activities where the pressure is off, creating a buffer zone from the everyday chaos. Those of us who feed on this energy boost often opt for the opposite; staying at the desk, working longer and focusing on producing, producing, producing. No energy is gained, fatigue only worsens.

Solitary – Time alone, perhaps with selected music, but often in silence, perhaps walking, away from the hubbub. Those of us who feed on this energy boost often opt for staying in the hubbub to get more done, to forcibly work it out, to find out more and more. No energy gained, fatigue continues to mount.

Treat yourself to a trial run with of each of these four actions over the next week and evaluate which one (or more) delivers the most clear and clean boost. Then commit to including a full dose in your day-to-day routine each week. You will notice the difference in your thinking, sense of priorities, clarity, and your ability to relax, be creative and work faster.

19. SIMPLIFY YOUR OVERWHELM

"Simplicity is the ultimate sophistication."

Leonardo da Vinci (1452-1519)

Overwhelm: to bury or drown beneath a huge mass of something, especially water.

We all have a relationship with being overwhelmed, and the water metaphor actually extends to describe my own. When I have heaps to do, to think about, to decide, to clear, it's as if I am submerged. My physical and mental ability to move seems slower, I feel weighed down and every way I turn there is more. It doesn't go away!

Even if your company isn't going through an existentially extreme moment such as merger, acquisition or other significant change, the chances are that at some time or another everything has become labelled urgent. Meetings are habitually scheduled so that you simply *have* to attend, and your time choices diminish. There is more information being created that you simply *have* to absorb.

This is where *being overwhelmed* graduates to over*load*, and ultimately, *over*!

A coaching client asked me to help her adjust her 'overwhelmed' attitude. She was ready to take a different approach to the pointless and ineffective 'work longer' approach. The dictionary definitions provoked my thinking.

1. Being overwhelmed is 'to be submerged'.

Being submerged means oxygen can be restricted. When you experience overwhelm it causes shortening of breath, tightening of the chest, hunching (perhaps over the desk). You are reducing the flow of air. This seriously changes your physiology and reduces your productivity and ability to think creatively and freely, as the brain shifs to survival mode and shuts down non-essential services.

When submerged, engage breathing apparatus. Set an alarm or some kind of reminder to pause every 15 minutes and take 5-10 deep inhalations and slow exhalations. You will notice the difference.

When submerged, the immediate environment is all you can see. Stop what you are doing, change your position, go talk to someone, and take two minutes to consider where you are, what you've achieved in the day so far and what is now most important.

2. Being overwhelmed is 'to be weighed down'.

When new weights are added to a system or a person without any corresponding change, there is a displacement of energy, or increase in strain. This needs to go somewhere and can manifest itself, ironically, as a 'snap'. The weight (or overwhelm items) are still there but no longer supported and have become scattered. You then work on the scattered pile of tasks in a haphazard way, making no real impression on the original volume, but become visibly busier, exhausted and straining in the process.

There are a number of ways I have been able to help people and teams increase their capacity in the workplace without extending (sometimes even reducing) the hours they work. It takes guts to pause, step back and simplify the situation.

To support more weight a bar needs to be strengthened. For you it means completing and going beyond delegation, reprioritization and task elimination. It means taking some personal care actions: rest, refuelling, relaxation, fitness training. Match what needs to be done with those who are naturally more efficient at doing those things, sharing tasks more widely across the team.

Too often being overwhelmed is not noticed or acted upon soon enough and the remedies have little effect when you are in too deep! The simplest way through being overwhelmed is to get used to noticing its tell-tale signs and then – individually or as a team – pause, consider the 'submerged' and 'weighed down' sections above and begin again.

20. THREE SIMPLE STEPS TO SOMEWHERE

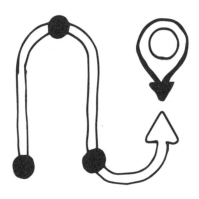

"Most people never run far enough on their first wind to find out if they've got a second. Give your dreams all you've got and you'll be amazed at the energy that comes out of you."

William James (1842-1910)

It will sound obvious and you will agree, intellectually at least, but getting somewhere essentially involves three steps:

1. Deciding where you want to go.

2. Realizing where you are now.

3. Setting off.

If any one of the three steps isn't taken, the journey is absolutely flawed from the start.

Your personal and business circumstances may often become so busy that you slip into 'merely existing' mode. In this mode you are focused only on getting things done, but not actually moving consistently in any one direction. And you may also be pretty good at justifying the situation. "I'll sort it out in the next gap..." "It'll be alright when..." "This is my job, life is like this..."

A phrase I am perhaps guilty of over-using in my workshops and speaking events is this call to action: "Nothing Changes Unless Something Changes." If you don't take some kind of new action, you'll be stuck in a version of today's mire in two months' or maybe even two years' time.

Let me draw your attention to step one:

1. Deciding where you want to go.

This crucial question demands time and focus to enhance clarity, and it's really difficult to do it alone. The more work you put in here, despite what your brain chatter may say, the faster you will move toward your goal.

If you are going to embark on this alone, consider carving out 30 minutes this week and go somewhere where you won't be disturbed. For the first 15 minutes simply write about what success means to you.

Some examples might include:

1. Time freedom.
2. Spending freedom.
3. Space (to live, move, write, relax).
4. Increased income.
5. Life being organized around you.
6. Hassle-free.
7. Doing what you enjoy and are good at.

For the second 15 minutes relax into the chair, and let your mind go to the place you have just described, where you are enjoying all that success. As you conclude your reflections, note down any additional insights you may have had, fold the paper up, file it and let go of the whole experience.

Do the same thing one week later, with a new sheet of paper.

And, if you're up for it, repeat this exercise a third time yet a week later. You will, by now, have clarity and have initiated an unstoppable wave of change-thinking that will take you toward your more clearly defined destination.

Taking time to consider your second and third steps ('Realizing where you are now' and 'Setting off') becomes significantly easier when you have clarity, passion and excitement about where you are headed.

2. Realizing Where You Are Now

Consider all the elements of your present situation. This is your start point. What is easy? What is difficult? What are you attracting (conversations, events, people)? What resources do you have, or have access to?

3. Setting Off

This sounds obvious, but I have met many who, even with clarity of destination and an awareness of where they are now, remain stuck and don't get moving. Just start! Read material about your destination, meet people, join blogs, attend seminars. Get involved, create daily actions. Make it easy to keep moving.

Other *Simple Notes* in this book also attend and inspire action with these deceptively powerful steps.

21. URGENTIA

*"Act as if what you do makes
a difference. It does."*

William James (1842-1910)

When evaluating your tasks, intentions, goals and to-do lists, etc.,
the Eisenhower Method is a trusted and well-used maxim that's
applied in almost every time-management lesson or programme.
I'm sure you know it and can recite the points it seeks to make. It
is simply obvious, isn't it?

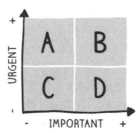

I'll remind you:

Identify all the tasks, commitments and actions in which you are involved and categorize them into the four boxes in the diagram above.

Assess the degree to which they are urgent (looming deadline or immediate requirement to be completed) and the degree to which they are important (developing and evolving yourself and the environment around you, solving bigger challenges, leading to your goals or greater success).

The best practise principle is to:

Work on the Urgent and Important first (*Box B*).

Work on the Not Urgent but Important box second (*Box D*).

Handle the Urgent, Unimportant quadrant in new ways (*Box A*).

Avoid Box C, Neither Urgent nor Important.

This 2×2 method comes into most of my coaching conversations. Amid today's constant volume of requests, emails, messages, notifications, meetings, projects, new possibilities, distractions, games, texts and social networking, people can unknowingly drift into a state of 'Urgentia'.

Urgentia is my word to describe a loss of awareness of actual important thinking and actions. Instead, everything that grabs your focus is laced with unspecified urgency.

Doubt and fear of failure have led to many people forcing the priority of tasks in business situations by artificially upping the urgency. I notice this immediately in commercial environments – the almost intangible controlled chaos is in a way, almost physically palpable!

Extreme Urgentia drives you to seek some sort of relief from a mixed dose of unimportant distractions. Things that aren't important simply aren't important. Ideally you shouldn't spend excessive time (and it's perhaps worth defining specifically what 'excessive' might be for you) on them. Your evolved self should eliminate them entirely.

In today's busy environment, you may be told by many that everything is now in Box B (Urgent and Important). Culturally, it may even have become accepted as a truth in your workplace. Most of the time this is not actually true. What may have happened – without you or those around you being consciously aware of it – is that you have become addicted to the buzz of the Urgent. You are suffering from 'Urgentia'.

Your many electronic devices are, by their nature, urgent. These include phones, especially mobiles, texts (even more so), email, message alerts and so on. Add to this the everyday hyped urgency of our media (TV, radio, web and printed press) and advertisements that scream for your attention and action NOW. Is it any wonder that we have ended up with an environment in which urgency rules? These are almost all in toxic Box A (the scale of urgency masks the fact that they may be absolutely unimportant).

Today you have more choices available to you than ever before – you are capable of taking empowered self-development steps in any moment you choose. Changing your business and personal life dramatically is a real and attainable option. But so often you don't. These types of action are always important and not urgent (precious Box D). They don't shout and scream; they require you to be measured, considered, conscious and deliberate. Time spent here always pays back, but it is lost to the 'red-alert' urgency lists.

Box D enjoys only fleeting moments of attention as your diary fills (or gets filled) with the urgent stuff. And without noticing, you are caught idling in Box C, convincing yourself that whatever you are doing is important, when really it isn't. It's simply not urgent and you have been enjoying the non-urgency of it. The same relaxed option awaits you in the important Box D as soon as you focus on it and lay into the tasks!

Urgentia is not big or clever, even though it feels like it when we are caught up in it. Bizarrely, when people are in the state of Urgentia, they appear more important than those working on the truly important things! Urgentia leads to missed goals, slipped deadlines, frantic over-productivity (of possibly irrelevant outputs), excessive stress and anxiety... and the feeling of no progress despite what seems to be immense effort.

So, what is a simple way to cure Urgentia?

Start an audit this week of where you have spent your time. Broadly mark against each period or task where it fell in the diagram shown on page 65.

Ask yourself the question, "Was this task truly important to me, my goals and aspirations?" Begin again, deliberately. Handle the urgent and do the important. Book time, reserve the space and take whatever action moves you forward in the direction of your goals.

Be deliberate and purposeful carving out time and space to focus on an important not 'urgent item'. It *will* meet resistance, but see it through.

While you are in your audit/noticing phase, keep an eye on how urgency is used around you. 'Buy now before it's too late,' 'Today only,' 'Last few remaining' – feel the adrenaline spike these provoke in you. Notice it and breathe through it. Choose calm!

22. SIX OF ONE, HALF A DOZEN OF THE OTHER

"Whether you think you can or that you can't, you are usually right."
Henry Ford (1863-1947)

'The above expression is one of many that were coined through the ages to encourage a balanced view of a situation. So, on the basis of my profound belief that your journey through life is as much about remembering as it is about learning anew, I shall bring the phrase back into focus.

Let me start with the assertion that when you think the world or a certain set of circumstances is against you, then it probably is. Such thinking leads to feeling less powerful and less positive.

You are more likely to be tense, for sustained periods of time. You smile less, frown more, grit your teeth and sit hunched over. You are more reluctant to change anything. And perhaps most noticeably, you over-react to situations, often disproportionately and inappropriately.

On the opposite side of the equation, if you think that the world and your place in it are absolutely ideal, then they probably are. You feel powerful, positive, confident and expansive. You allow yourself to relax deeply and often. You smile all the time, walk taller and notice more. You are willing to change virtually anything and are open to new thinking. And perhaps most noticeably, you allow situations to be what they are, and consider and respond to them appropriately. There is no fight or resistance.

Whatever is happening with you right now – at home, at work or simply inside you – just is. There will be 'six of one, half a dozen of the other', all the time, and you get to decide which half grabs your attention.

Over my years of coaching, it has become abundantly clear among my clients which of the two states allowed them to achieve more, where transformation and transition occurred faster, and where a fabulous grin was easier to muster.

The pragmatically powerful 'six of one' truism is a reminder-tool to nudge your thinking into a more helpful state. When you are noticing only the wrong six, it compounds, and more than six seem to turn up to prove it. Seek the other six, and simplify your situation in that moment.

For the next week I challenge you to notice your state, and on the occasions when you are facing the not-so-nice six ask yourself and write down answers to the following:

1.   What could be the 'half a dozen of the other' here?

2.   What might be/could be good about this?

3.   How might this be helpful for me or others?

Keep asking the same questions until something comes to mind, particularly in the toughest situations when they show up... as they surely will.

23. TOLERATIONS

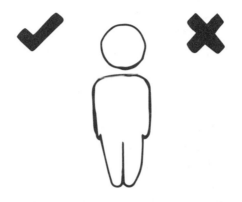

*"It isn't the mountain ahead that wears you out
– it's the grain of sand in your shoe."*

Robert Service (1874-1958)

Tolerations are all those annoying, aggravating, frustrating, energy-draining things that you are putting up with, or suffering through. They drain time, money, other resources, love, patience and so on. They take up space and consume energy. When your toleration count is high, your energy levels and reserves are frequently depleted, your enthusiasm wanes quickly, your resilience is low and everyday challenges hit you too hard.

Tolerations are born of the actions of others, situations, unmet needs, crossed boundaries, loose ends and unfinished past business, frustrations, problems and even your own behaviour.

They could include a cluttered desk, family members who do not respect your decisions, clients who don't pay on time, a dripping tap that annoys you, a door that sticks to the frame. And if that tap has been dripping or that door has been sticking for months, or even years, it has a direct (and negative) impact on your ability to feel good. Remember the power of that tiny grain of sand.

You may even have repeatedly told yourself the story that these things are just part of your life and there's no point paying any attention to them as they're not quite at that point where you *have* to do something about them, and so you just get on with the rest of your everyday business.

There is a wonderful opportunity for you to access huge boosts to your energy, productivity and general 'feel good' state, by following a gentle process of becoming toleration-free.

Simply recognize that tolerations exist, notice and acknowledge them and begin to eliminate as many as possible. By sweeping these away, your path to reaching your goals will become clearer, unhindered and easier to traverse.

Step One – Write down everything that you are currently tolerating. The most common areas where they show up are in our environments (rooms in the home, work spaces, the car); in our relationships (family, friends, colleagues, customers, suppliers); in our events (meetings, policies, procedures, regular scheduled activity); and in what we own or don't yet own (the state of our possessions, clothes, equipment and the absence of what we actually require to be effective). Keep adding to this list as you think of the tolerations in your life.

Step Two – Start sweeping them away, one at a time. Begin with the easy ones. If you get stuck, get support.

You will be pleasantly surprised at the positively disproportionate euphoric effect each sweep of your toleration broom will cause.

To get yourself in motion, I challenge you to start that list right now and then pick three items from your list (easy ones first, to create some momentum) and wipe them out. You'll feel so energized by doing so that you'll carry on, well on your way to becoming toleration-free!

24. BRINGING GOALS TO LIFE

*"People with goals succeed because they know where
they are going. It's as simple as that."*

Earl Nightingale (1921-1989)

At some point in your career you will have been told that you should
use goals to drive you to new results, raise your game or capitalize
on your potential. It's no surprise, then, that there are hundreds
of 'Goal-Getter' or 'Goal-Maker' products, processes, programmes
and coaching supports available to help.

I have often spent time thinking about my goals. Do I actually have
any? What was my route to get what I now have, where and who
I now am – was it goal-fuelled? To be honest, my answers were

inconclusive, so I set about simplifying this process, which is my recommended way through such situations.

Put simply, goals come to life when the following mental states exist:

Clarity – I am clear about them.

Belief – I believe I will achieve them (even if they are hugely stretching or even seemingly impossible).

Action – I act as if the goal were true and had come about already. Perhaps you have only one or two of these steps in place and the others are low-priority or non-existent. It doesn't mean the goal won't be achieved, just that it may take longer, or be achieved with less clarity or accuracy.

Score each of the three mental states from one to ten and multiply the result. The range then is from one to one thousand.

Where any of the scores are zero, the obvious result is always zero (it will not be achieved), no matter how high the other scores may be.

Where the scores are low, work in just one of the mental state areas, not all three simultaneously. This focus will speed up your journey to the goal.

My scores have often been low in clarity, always high in belief and variable in action. Any enhancements I make simply accelerate new results for me.

Here are some thoughts to get your focus work under way:

For Clarity write down your current goal, no matter how ambiguous it may be at first. Talk to others about similar goals, read about the topic. Rewrite and refine your goal statement often.

For Belief note what is true about the goal already, with even the tiniest proof points. Research others who have achieved similar goals from tougher starting points than yours. Spend time with or reading about those who have achieved.

For Action (as if the goal were already achieved) shift your behaviour from being lacking or chasing to a sense of assuredness. How might you behave when you have achieved the goal, how might you walk, talk, etc? And be that.

25. EXPECTATION PLAYLIST

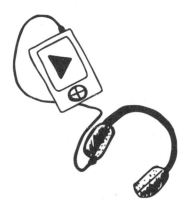

*"Do not spoil what you have by desiring what you have not;
remember that what you now have was once among the things
you only hoped for."*

Robert Service (1874-1958)

In a coaching call I invited a client to talk to me as if from the end
of the week, looking back.

Immediately, she described an expected set of outcomes that she
knew, in advance, she wouldn't feel great about. Reality was inform-
ing her range of results and feelings. But she had a choice. It was
only Tuesday, four full working days to go before that Friday outcome.
What would she like to say? What feeling state would she want to

have, given the choice? In spite of the apparent reality of what might occur she began to describe a new expectation.

When we caught up a week later, the result was indeed different. It was not her initial expectation – it was in fact better, improved and just as she had set the desired outcome. She enjoyed a feeling of contentment and success that were definitely not on the first agenda.

Does this happen to you? Of course it does, perhaps more often than you realize. You are rolling toward a set of outcomes and resulting feelings; an unconscious, but just as powerful, expectation. Your mood and attitudes are pre-determined, like a DJ who has already chosen the playlist before the programme begins. Your expectations will come to pass, unless you change the playlist.

Start with thinking about your default expectation, then upgrade it (in spite of reality). Remind yourself daily and your attitude muscles will do the rest.

26. RETREAT

"Nothing is a waste of time if you use the experience wisely."
Auguste Rodin (1840-1917)

The double, almost contrasting, meaning of the word 'retreat' has, for me, always been worthy of investigation and contemplation.

To retreat is to go back, reverse or return. It also refers to an escape, a time away from everyday hustle and bustle to reflect and review.

I suggest you apply both definitions as potential strategies to simplify complicated and difficult situations you face.

When I meet with tough circumstances and it feels like I am wading through mud, one of my first actions is to press on, try harder, work longer, and throw more at it. This inevitably proves to be an ineffective strategy, leading to an energy- and fun-sapping time... and I just don't like it.

My challenge to you is to consider where you are meeting resistance. What seems heavy going, hard work? Then, following on the first definition, *retreat* – go back in the other direction, take time to reflect or simply take a completely and utterly different route. Retrace your last three steps or series of activities. Could they be begun again, differently?

Then, following on the second definition, *retreat* again. This time remove yourself from the difficult, challenging or complicated situation. Move to somewhere calm, serene and spacious for a specific period of time (an hour or more, depending on the degree of complexity you are facing) and review as much about your current situation as you can. Ask yourself:

How did I get here?

Where am I currently headed, following this path?

What or where is my retreat easy/difficult/meeting resistance?

Who has experience here?

What other options are available to me (given sufficient time or money)?

Shake yourself off and return to your challenge. You will have had, or will have set in motion, new insights and thinking to simplify and shift gears.

27. BECOME FRUSTRATION-FREE

"Everything that irritates us about others can lead us to a better understanding of ourselves."

Carl Jung (1875-1961)

You're a busy person. There is a lot happening, communication is fast and comes at you and from you through multiple sources. The everyday choices about where to focus and what you choose to get done seem to multiply.

Increasingly, getting things done depends on your connection and collaboration with others who are likely experiencing the same plethora of options and make completely different decisions than you.

Outcome = frustration, and a widening gap between potentially helpful collaborative relationships.

Frustration with yourself and the choices you did or didn't make. Frustration with the situations and contexts in which you find yourself. Frustration with others for all of those reasons and more.

How does frustration manifest itself in you, and how do your behaviour and mood change?

You may feel drained, and perhaps angry and bitter at times, and it just doesn't feel good.

I have continually proved to myself that when you feel good you perform better, think faster, think more creatively and attract more opportunities and desirable events (which feels good!). So my suggestion to release your frustration is to shift to a more empowered state.

Here's a method you can immediately use to neutralize frustrations.

Simon's Frustration Neutralizer Method:

Grab a pen, find a new page in the back of your notebook or the blank space at the end of this chapter and write down on the left hand side the top five things that are frustrating you. Just the frustration, not the why.

Alongside each, begin a new sentence using the same subject description, replacing 'frustrated by' with 'it's great that' and allow your creative brain to come up with the reasons why the situation could, just possibly, be great.

How does this work? It shifts your mood and attitude from negative to at least neutral. From there you will feel better, release more of your creative thinking power and create the space for more and more compelling reasons why things are okay to come to mind. Choose the serene response.

And to be frustration-free?

First, give yourself clear and unambiguous permission to be frustration-free (you may be addicted to it, expect it and ready yourself to be frustrated every day!).

Second, stop talking about your frustrations, which in effect fuels them, keeps them in your consciousness and bringing them to life.

Third, keep working with the Frustration Neutralizer Method.

28. BOOST PERSONAL PRODUCTIVITY

*"The more efficient a force is, the more silent
and the more subtle it is."*

Mahatma Gandhi (1869-1948)

Many people tend to find themselves in the middle of significantly increased numbers of lengthy 'To-Do' lists. The projects in which they are involved are increasing while the resources available, at best, remain the same.

Perhaps you have found yourself in such a situation, feeling the pressure to achieve and become increasingly competitive. Yet the distractions are many, the number of meetings multiplies, unanswered messages accumulate.

Any tangible, productive progress is often only partial, disappointingly slow and likely to compound your frustration.

Here is a simple, three-step tip to boost your productivity by helping you become more deliberate. For the next two weeks take the following steps at the start of your working day (and I repeat the importance of doing this at the start – rather than at the middle or end of your day – as you are setting in action some crucial attitude shifts).

First, pause for 10 minutes. Sit at rest with no distractions.

Second, among all the things you've got to do, consider which three things you would really like to make progress on or complete today (they don't even have to be deadline-dependent).

Third, write them down on the back of one of your business cards (or any blank card) and keep this with you, visible, all day.

This card is your absolute focus. Regardless of the meetings in your schedule, or the calls you make or take, the three things on the card are your purpose for the day. Your day is not over until they are done. If you complete them early, enjoy the rest of the day in a relaxed state of 'completion'. Anything else you get done is purely a bonus.

Repeat for a concerted period of time (minimum 10 working days, maximum 20). You will have completed between 30 and 60 significant productivity steps, which I'm convinced you would not achieve without this sort of focus. You will otherwise be at the beck and call of everyday tasks, demands and miscellaneous distractions that may not have any impact on your important personal productivity.

29. DOWNWIND

"The fishermen know that the sea is dangerous and the storm terrible, but they have never found these dangers sufficient reason for remaining ashore."

Vincent van Gogh (1853-1890)

After returning from a week's sailing in the Baltic, I was full of stories and analogies and ready to dispense them both liberally, as my sailing trips inevitably inspire me to do.

One parallel that struck me clearly on this particular trip was the challenge of working with the direction of the wind and, while it sounds obvious, how it affects the route to your destination, in ways that may not be entirely obvious.

It is rare in life and rarer at sea to simply select a destination and head in a straight line to it. Fluctuating conditions, like those you experience in your workplace, mean that a direct route between points A and B is rarely an option. If you simply press on, you will feel like you are moving only slowly, if at all, toward your goal. You may have to adjust both your sails and your course.

On one particular day in the Baltic, heading to our destination would have meant having the wind directly behind us. This sounds swell and fast, doesn't it? Just fill the sails and off we go in a straight line. It can be fast but in reality is a dangerous 'point-of-sail' and difficult for the boat to maintain course safely. The powerful push of the wind in the tail places immense strain on the sails, the mast and the potential widow-making boom, which holds the mainsail. The preferred setting was away from the wind, first to the west, then back to the east, extending our journey in distance but using the sailboat more efficiently, the way it was designed, safely and still maintaining a good speed.

How often do the conditions in your world seem absolutely perfect (the wind is behind you) but the experience becomes nerve-wracking, with events happening so fast around you? The reckless, who stay on that course, may indeed finish fast but often attract damage – to relationships, to projects, to workloads and to quality. The worried turn off course, and avoid the conditions completely, slowing right down and missing the opportunity for pace, growth, improvement, change or project progress.

The most powerful choice would be to adjust your course slightly, in effect to tack left and right. At work this might be in the form of a rapid review of your short- and long-term goals.

Could my goals move or be different, or even be put on hold?

What might now be in range?

What standards could we maintain or reduce in this period?

Perhaps set some short-term goals that you would not normally consider, and engage in more frequent, rapid reviews and re-evaluations, of the situation, your speed and progress, assessing what's important (quality, communication, relationships). Pause (see the *'Pause' Simple Note*) and tune in to your intuition. It may also mean shifting roles within the team for a few weeks, changing the focus and challenging ingrained habits.

Whatever the conditions for you in the weeks ahead, consider your heading and where the wind is coming from or taking you. Are you in a downwind phase? What short-term changes could you make to maximize your safety, enjoyment and results?

30. HOW TEAMS CAN ACHIEVE FIVE-OUT-OF-FIVE

"Treat people as if they were what they ought to be, and you help them to become what they are capable of being."
Johann Wolfgang von Goethe (1749-1832)

While working with a team of talented, motivated and busy project managers, I was intrigued by a regular part of their weekly team meeting – a 'temperature check'. Each team member was invited to rate how they felt in terms of connection to the team, current happiness level, etc., and give those feelings a score of one to five.

Somewhat predictably, the scores ranged from two (the person who was overwhelmed and swamped in projects) through to assured threes and a four (the optimist with an effervescent attitude who just loves the challenge and enjoys every day).

I took this opportunity to pose the silly and simple question of what might warrant a score of five.

The answers were interesting and began to unlock the possibility that a 'five' might actually exist. Each team member viewed a 'five' situation quite differently. For some it was about a sense of completion, for others it was recognition, acknowledgement, noticeable impact, smiling more, learning, connecting, celebrating, and so on. Much of the criteria for a score of five was off the agenda and considered out of reach. No surprise then that no one considered the possibility of having a five-out-of-five experience.

I even sensed a hint of guilt about the thought of letting oneself experience an indulgent five. How ridiculous. I go to work seeking five-out-of-five days and most of the most successful people with whom I have worked have more five-days than any other number.

Is it simply a shift of mindset? Perhaps.

In order to move this particular team on and continue to open up the possibility of a five in its members' lives it was time to simplify.

Rather than create a vision of a five-day streak, how about a five-out-of-five moment, or hour, or morning. What might those circumstances be? We worked through a few questions and came up with a personal recipe for each member of the team.

So my challenge to you is to consider the possibility of a five-out-of-five day in your world. It needs to start well and be focused on what leads you to that 'five' feeling.

In order to create the possibility of you actually experiencing a 'five-day' first consider the conditions:

How would you start that day?

Where would you focus first?

Who would you spend time with?

What or who would you avoid?

Go on, simplify and create some five-out-of-five experiences, string them together and soon whole days will feel great.

31. THOUGHT MANAGEMENT 101

"The soul is dyed the colour of its thoughts. Think only on those things that are in line with your principles and can bear the light of day. The content of your character is your choice. Day by day, what you do is who you become."

Heraclitus (535-475 BC)

Have you ever wondered why you think what you think? And whether there actually is a direct link between what you think about and what turns up in your life?

On my journeys I have met evolved souls who enjoy such a deeply serene place that they can exert incredible control over their thoughts and seem able to create what they want to maintain and sustain their serenity. But if you are still in a thought-evolution phase, controlling and managing your thoughts is a difficult task.

In simple terms your thoughts are triggered by the plethora of stimuli to which you are exposed. Colours, people, sounds, food, body position, places, smells. Before you begin the hard work of managing all this there is a simple step you can immediately take to improve your results.

Choose the thoughts you want to follow.

Without 'thinking about your thinking' you can find yourself focusing on an ill-desired thought for several minutes. And in doing so you activate the thought, give it life, creative space and your mood and attitude shift with it.

If you follow a positive thought, you automatically expand it with additional, linked thoughts. Your mood and attitude shift that way too.

Which feels better? Which thought, when followed, leads to new positive thoughts, ideas, and the ability to notice opportunities that may otherwise have passed you by?

I challenge you to practise this exercise today. When a thought comes up that you don't like, simply let it go – stop thinking about it beyond the point of noticing it. Initiate a new and better thought (like the view from your window or the best thing about your next hour) and follow that, for at least two minutes. Then consider how you feel.

And as a bonus to this exercise, consider what thoughts you cause in those around you. Are they positive? What reactions do you cause? What might they be thinking about as a result of you and your actions, words and attitudes?

Keep it simple and follow the good thoughts.

32. HAVE YOU LEFT A PAN OF MILK ON?

"Waste not fresh tears over old griefs."

Euripides (480-406 BC)

Have you ever experienced that nagging sensation as you leave home or the office that something important has been left undone?

For years, whenever my family has left home for a weekend or a holiday, the flippant question, 'Have you left a pan of milk on the boil?' is asked as a nudge to remind us to rack our brains to make sure nothing obvious has been forgotten before we set off.

I have noticed the energetic drain that this type of uncertainty and incompleteness brings. I have noticed it in myself and in my clients.

When your concentration is impaired, part of your mind being focused elsewhere – on possible pans of milk – you act this out in uncertain ways, even in tasks in which you should have certainty. This feeling of incompleteness is annoying, uncomfortable and, quite simply, holding you back.

I have also noticed that the sensation can still be occurring at deeper levels beyond the obvious milk pan situation.

Small, almost forgotten, unfinished items, from the immediate past or more distant times, gnaw away and reduce your potential to feel great during the day.

These 'incompletes' might be unpaid bills, outstanding conversations or pending decisions, partially completed projects, gratitude not given or not received, and so on. The list can be enormous and somehow our brain holds the disappointment that we won't be able to complete them all today.

Assuming you do actually want to feel great and operate at five-out-of-five more often, you have two choices:

1. Say to yourself that whatever is undone is the way it is, you are happy that it is so and you are ready to be fully present now, unaffected by whatever is incomplete. While this is a quick and easy way forward, you probably have an active and investigative mind that may return to scanning your memory banks, thus bringing back the energy-draining items.

2. The second option is to grasp the list, get explicit with what is gnawing at you, even (and especially) the tiny, subtle items. Look at the list and make a decision here and now which items can be completed immediately, which can go into your diary for the week ahead and which are no longer relevant to you and can be cast away. This clearance strategy might mean a batch of emails, texts or phone calls are necessary to wrap up unfinished conversations or open-ended discussions.

Good luck with your milk pan strategy; you will be astounded by how good it feels when you take a step forward in this way. You may not tie up all those loose ends but the purposeful way with which you raise your awareness and your action will diminish many previously undetected energy drains.

33. PERSONAL BOARD OF DIRECTORS

"In everyone's life, at some time, our inner fire goes out. It is then burst into flame by an encounter with another human being. We should all be thankful for those people who rekindle the inner spirit."

Albert Schweitzer (1875-1965)

Often, senior executives and leaders carry complex decisions around with them and find themselves tackling these alone. The real truth is, you are never alone.

A reliable and extremely effective method of decision support is to reconnect with the people who have influenced your path so far. Be they alive or dead, real or fictitious, advice and guidance can be garnered from these respected and admired influencers.

Grab a pen and paper and contemplate the following:

- Who are the five people (more if you like) who have had an impact on your career, decisions and life choices? People you have admired, respected or perhaps even emulated, copied?

- Consider each of the names on your list and think about the influence they had on you, the circumstance and the outcome. Note down three words or short phrases that describe this. These people are the first non-exec directors of 'You PLC'.

- Next, bring to mind the most challenging problem you are facing. A decision that you have not yet reached, an issue you are still contemplating or words you have yet to speak. This may be interfering with your sleep or impacting your general wellbeing.

Randomly choose two people from your 'You PLC' list and 'ask' their view of your topic. What advice do they have?

Remember, you don't have to take the advice, just consider the different viewpoint, and how it might address your situation. Does it move you on, is your influencer's view something you could take and adapt, does it present more questions or is there something to be made from the combination of insights you receive?

You get to choose your board of directors. You can even sack them and replace them! I have worked with clients who have added family members, admired fictional characters, and public figures who they understand, have read about, met and respect.

Enjoy your next board meeting, and keep it simple.

34. UPGRADE YOUR INNER CRITIC

"Courage is what it takes to stand up and speak;
courage is also what it takes to sit down and listen."

Sir Winston Churchill (1874-1965)

I relish the opportunity and challenge of public speaking, particularly at business conferences. At an event some years ago, my audience-impact challenge was to instil a lasting, positive change to attitude and self-belief... in 45 minutes. The audience were going through massive organizational change and operating in an unstable marketplace. My topic was 'Personal Resilience'.

I was very aware going into this event, more than normally, of the power of my inner voice. The frightened, damning Inner Critic!

As I prepared my talk, the voice spoke (loudly), full of doubt, and from that fearful place that forms and poses unhelpful questions: Will I have any impact at all? Is the content right? Is there enough or too much?

The neutralizing force in the prep stage was my mentor. In her own grounded and pragmatic way she reminded me of how I had faced similar challenges and succeeded. She bluntly told me to stop worrying and get on with it. You'll be fine, she said, and the content is great.

On the day of the event I met other presenters, and was aware of my Inner Critic comparing me to them, scraping up the embers of doubt back into flame. Will I actually be credible? Who do I think I am? They are so much more professional than me...

I'm glad that this event took place, as it was the opportunity for me to permanently upgrade my Inner Critic.

Maybe you have an active Inner Critic too – one that activates whenever you have a significant event ahead, or a project to complete, a message to deliver, etc. The Critic speaks from the scared ego, pulling you back to a low-risk posture; to the skittish "sometimes doing nothing is best" mindset. It may accelerate nerves and anxiety, and fill you with doubt.

But this doesn't have to be the case. There are many coping methods I have used and worked with. A more permanent change is to upgrade the Critic instead of just quietening that annoying inner voice.

1. First, get explicit about and evaluate your expectations for the talk. What are your hopes and intentions for it? What could they be? This last question is difficult to answer if the Critic is already in conversation. However, when asked early enough,

it will have positive impact and can raise your sights and ultimately your game.

2. Next, tune in to the inner voices. The Critic may be yattering, but so too will another thought section of your mind – the Encourager – albeit much more quietly. Every time the Critic makes a comment, notice how you feel. Physiologically, you slump. This is not good. And if you begin your presentation (or whatever you are about to face) in this state you are more likely to stumble, stutter, err and fluff. When your Encourager makes a comment, and you actually hear it, you may not instantly become full of joy, but you will be calmer.

Pay attention to both your Critic and your Encourager. Both are thought chains sourced from your emotional state regarding the event, channelling fear and doubt from the Critic; and hope and belief from the Encourager.

When the Critic makes a comment, don't listen. Choose another thought (often the absolute opposite) and keep thinking it. For extra help here read the *Thought Management 101' Simple Note*. You have to get in the way and change the inner story-telling.

Don't forget that you get to choose who you listen to and follow.

As with my experience with the Personal Resilience speech, within a few minutes of taking these two upgrade steps, the Critic generally upgrades itself and begins to help, not hinder. And the presentation went extremely well, thank you.

Keep calm and carry on!

35. LIBERATING THE GRIP OF 'OUGHT TO'

*"You will become as small as your controlling desire;
as great as your dominant aspiration."*

James Allen (1864-1912)

Your choices are vast, even though you may spend most of your time unaware of the available options as you follow the same habitual choosing process, perhaps harbouring a muffled complaint that things just don't seem to get better.

What presents itself to you, your everyday reality, is directly related to two things:

1.   What you think about (persistently).

2. The direction of travel (the actions you repeatedly take).

I often notice the gripping power of a particular underlying thought – one that, left untouched, saps your power and enjoyment, as you unconsciously think more of the same.

That is the 'ought to'.

Wrapped up in the decision-making unit inside your mind is a 'want to,' 'need to,' 'should do,' 'could do' and of course the mystifying and nebulous 'ought to'.

In order to feel better and enjoy a sense of progress, satisfaction and achievement, these thoughts require distilling before they mix together, fog your priorities and choices and get treated as the same, which they most certainly are not.

A simple distillation:

Want Tos – These rarely get enough of your time, and are instead put on a shelf, where you remain aware of them but downhearted that you haven't taken any inspired action on them. They embody enjoyment and provide access to more of your potential. Give them more focus immediately, carve out time and be assertive here.

Need Tos – These are often essential parts of your life. If you like them, go there. If you don't, outsource and/or automate them, but don't ignore them. If they truly need to get done, at some point you must require attention.

Should Dos – These are Need Tos with less power. Decide whether they can be upgraded to Need Tos or just let them go; they're taking up space and energy and drain you as quickly as they accumulate.

Could Dos – These are interesting and often more creative, forward-looking, positive change steps. Schedule some quality time and let your mind expand your Could Dos. They can be the catalyst for your future and deserve to be allowed some quality airtime.

Finding time here, and with the Want Tos, will differentiate you and your work from the rest (who won't find the time!).

Ought Tos – This is the category that intrigues me most of all. Ought Tos could be like any of the other four, but lie angrily dormant, niggling, causing you discomfort, and inhibit your belief system from making any progress at all.

What are the Ought Tos on your mind? Spend more time with relatives? Work out more? Eat better? Plan more? Get organized? Change a habit?

Ought Tos are often poorly categorized Wants, Needs, Shoulds or Coulds. Left alone, they drain you, but with immediate and regular sorting, your own well-being and personal evolution gain the clarity they require.

Here's a simple, liberating Ought to step:

Begin a list and spend the next week adding your Ought Tos as they come to mind.

Add four columns to the right of your Ought To list.

In the first, rate how important each could be to you, with a score from one to five (where five has the potential to be positively life-changing).

In the second column rate each in terms of how truly inspired you are right now to take action (with a score of five signifying absolutely yes, in this very moment!).

In the third column multiply the previous two numbers.

Identify and highlight the top three scores in your list. For your top three note a single action you could take today to move in the direction of, and liberate, your 'ought to' (add this in the fourth column).

Take that action – you will feel surprisingly good and will have generated new momentum in the direction of your inner, previously entangled, desires.

The sooner you embark on this, the sooner your current reality will change. Revisit this exercise every three months to dramatically and permanently transform your world.

36. SIMPLE MEDITATION

*"All of man's problems derive from our inability
to sit quietly in a room and do nothing."*

Blaise Pascal (1623-1662)

To meditate or to take steps to enhance mindfulness is now accepted in the mainstream of personal development. Meditation is a method to separate yourself from your thoughts and feelings in order to become fully aware.

It can have profound transformational results. And yet it eludes many who resist putting it into regular practice.

For years I resisted the concept of meditation as it required incense, a cross-legged posture and the chiming of Tibetan bowls, which left me sceptical and under-resourced.

What I have learned, however, is the power of simply *stopping* for even the shortest period of time, and allowing busy thinking to subside. This is the beginning of a meditative practice.

Brain research informs us that your mind operates at up to sixteen times faster than your body and your speech. So it is not surprising that we can sometimes become inextricably entangled in multiple-layer thinking, losing focus and, often, experiencing serious mental or physical fatigue.

Simple mediation is just that – simple. It doesn't require things like incense or soothing music (although they can enhance the experience as your practise evolves). It is about stopping conscious activity for as little as two minutes.

Here's a way to introduce simple meditation into your schedule this week:

Find a comfortable seat in as settled a location as possible, away from interruptions and peripheral noise.

Breathe in and out naturally, but a little slower and deeper than normal. Count out ten sets of an inhale and an exhale. Then, in your mind, slowly count back down from 10 to one.

Simply concentrate on your breathing and nothing else. Let thoughts come and go (sometimes picturing the number of each breath, one through to ten, as large as possible in your mind's eye helps).

That's it!

The busier you are, and the more cluttered your mind, the more difficult this challenge will be, but the greater the impact you will experience. On occasions you will lose track of your counting as you follow a thought. Begin again from one.

To astound yourself with the positive affects this stopping process can have, repeat this meditation exercise at the same time each day for a week. Get your mind and body used to the time and place... and simply STOP!

Simple.

37. RETURN ON INVESTMENT OF YOUR TIME

*"I expect to pass through this world but once.
Any good therefore that I can do, or any kindness
that I can show to any fellow creature, let me do
it now. Let me not defer or neglect it, for I shall
not pass this way again."*

William Penn (1644-1718)

Many of my clients have such packed schedules that they feel like they're being whipped along in a fast-flowing river, with little power to change direction. A frequent outcome is that some weeks they feel good (and inspired), to others they feel bad (and drained).

Are you leaving your outcome to fate, allowing the course, pace and flow of the river to have control?

Becoming more deliberate about where you invest your time can, in effect, become a tiller to steer your course along your river. Ask yourself:

Where do I spend my time?

What is the impact on me during those commitments?

Take last week as an example. Let's say, for argument's sake, you worked fifty hours. What was the split of your time across the following time-investment categories?

The Self – Time in your own space, unhindered, uninterrupted, focused or unfocused, reflecting or taking action, just time with yourself.

The Inspiring – With people or in places that inspire or motivate you, that provoke you to think differently, where you garner and expand new ideas, or feed your desire for reflective time.

The Norm – With people or in places that comprise your typical and everyday current 'norm' as you know it. Occasionally challenging, but where you are mostly in control of the situation with few surprises.

The Drain – With people, or places, or tasks that simply drain you and take your energy levels right down.

It doesn't take a master detective like Sherlock Holmes to make the link between your time investment and the feel-good or feel-bad outcomes.

Do the analysis, become aware, then shift your schedule, deliberately.

1. Minimize 'drain' time immediately.

2. Increase 'inspiring' time. This can take a little extra thought and effort as you seek out opportunities. Space will open up to do this in the next category.

3. Get some 'self-time' – now! Schedule it, protect it and expand upon it week after week. This is the key to unlocking your potential.

Be simply deliberate, or the river will take you where it wants to go, and not necessarily where you want to go.

38. SIMPLIFYING RESOLUTIONS

"If you want to find your past, look at your present.
If you want to know your future, look at your present."

Chinese Proverb

Although it is possible at any time of year, January is the greatest reason or nudge we have to make or begin a change, cease a bad habit or take action on that nagging subject we have always said we would.

According to the Opinion Corporation of Princeton, NJ:

- 62% of people make New Year's resolutions.

- 8% are always successful.

- 19% achieve resolutions every-other year.

- 49% have infrequent success.

- 24% never succeed and have failed on every resolution, every year.

That's 1 in 4 people who fail each and every time!

I have noticed that many people have acquired a level of flippant cynicism and acceptable failure regarding their ability to resolve (and resolve and resolve!).

Here are a few thoughts to simplify and perhaps inspire the change you truly desire – a chance to get through the fog of doubt, and the cynical doubt that you can change.

Don't have any resolutions – If you are reading this, then you are clearly interested in your development and on a path of resolution, not linked to January, or any other artificial resolution-ignition day.

Find the compulsion – What are the three compelling reasons why this resolution needs to happen? Write them down and remind yourself often (affix sticky notes to your PC monitor, write on the tiles in your shower, anything to keep them visible and in mind).

Spotlighting – Create a totem/poster/image of your situation with resolution complete. Use whatever you want: magazine cut-outs, drawings, physical objects. Keep this in a prime place, on view every day.

Choose one – Lots of evidence now suggests that humans can only point willpower in one direction at a time. So, just take one objective and make that your sole focus.

Make a regular appointment – Put a recurring 30-minute appointment in your diary every week, entitled Resolution-Review, to assess, review and revitalize your resolution.

Find a resolution buddy – Motivate them in exchange.

Follow the feeling – If during January or February it doesn't feel right, let it go. You may cause unnecessary pain by hanging on to what isn't actually right for you at this time.

Make it physical – Is there some physical/visual change you can make to signify the re-start? Maybe move your office around, clear out your wardrobe of clothes that no longer serve you, put your watch on the opposite wrist.

Automate It – Simplify and ease the action or the steps leading to the action, to the maximum extent that you can (if it is going to the gym more often, prepare several bags of kit ready and put them by the door or in the car).

Reward yourself – Set reward thresholds and, crucially, deliver on the rewards you promise yourself when the thresholds are met (not before!), for example a weekend away, a new phone etc.

May your resolve gain strength, and achievement become your norm.

39. WHAT ARE
YOU READING?

*"Be careful the environment you choose
for it will shape you; be careful the friends
you choose for you will become like them."*

W. Clement Stone (1902-2002)

What are you reading? It's just a question, but one worthy of an answer. During a normal week your attitude, mental state, mood and state of being are influenced by the many external stimuli to which you are exposed (deliberately, consciously or not).

Simply to accept what is coming at you, and to consume what is in front of you, is a perilous strategy. To be vaguely unaware of what is coming at you is a similarly dangerous strategy.

This *Simple Note* focuses specifically on what you read, and it equally applies to what you watch on TV, listen to on the radio, the conversations in which you are actively or passively involved, the places you visit, and so on.

I gave up reading a daily newspaper many years ago, as I began to notice that some of the content changed my mood, affecting the ensuing minutes or hours, or sometimes the whole day.

Yes, there will be stuff you need to read and absorb in order to help you in your profession, your career, to follow your passion or your interests. But everything else has no place for you. It will not disappear on its own; in fact the opposite is true. The volume of unsolicited, unhelpful, disempowering messages from multiple sources is increasing for everyone.

Observe yourself over the next week. After reading the online or printed press, blogs, vlogs, bulletins, etc. run an internal audit of your response mood: what articles remain in your thoughts, how do you feel about them?

If it doesn't feel good, give it up... now!

You are at your best when you feel good so stop spoiling the good stuff and reduce the inputs that take you off track.

Exercise your power of choice and read what takes you forward, inspires you or positively challenges you, and leave the rest.

40. THE 3-4-3 STRATEGY

*"The road to happiness lies in two simple principles:
find what it is that interests you and that you can do well,
and when you find it put your whole soul into it – every bit
of energy and ambition and natural ability you have."*

John D. Rockefeller III (1906-1978)

Besides being, in my opinion, the best soccer formation, 3-4-3 has become a successful way to shift my clients' behaviour to helping them spend more time doing and being what they are designed to do and be.

When I meet a team, a client or participants in a workshop or conference, I often ask how much of their time could be described as being at their best. How effective do they consider themselves to be at that particular moment? Then out pour the stories about the volume of work, meetings, etc., that get in the way of operating at their peak. And they offer up some brilliant justifications for why most of their working days are spent this way.

The 3-4-3 strategy works like this.

Think about everything involved in being you and doing your job. Everything!

Top Three – Approximately 30% of what you do or get involved in will be what makes you go "ooh". You are great at it; time seems to slip past when you're in the act of doing it; no one else could ever do it quite the way you do, to your standards; when you've completed these things you actually feel better, not tired; it may take time, but it certainly doesn't seem to take effort. These are the things that, if you spent all your time doing them and not the other stuff, you would be an unstoppable machine!

Bottom Three – At the other end of the spectrum are 30% of the things that you are poor at. You probably put them off until they build up, fester and shout at you. When you are working on them, you feel drained and uninspired and your mind wanders. You begin to detest the task and everything and everyone associated with it; you look for and take any distraction from it; you're inefficient at these things and they take an achingly disproportionate length of time.

Middle Four – In the middle you've got the rest: 40% of the things you do are okay; part of the job, expected and known. You know they've got to be done and you get them done.

The juicy opportunity for you is to get to a point where you are aware of the distinction between the top three and the bottom three items.

Make an active decision to spend more time doing your top three – don't put them off, waiting until you've suffered and done the nasty things. Maybe consider a compromise and do one of the middle four for every one of the top three.

These top three items are what you will be praised for, rewarded for, thanked for. People will talk about you and your way with these top three item things. This is the essence of you, your talents and why you are here.

Next, make an active decision to spend less time on the bottom three. Don't kid yourself that everything will be fine when these are completed, because it won't. It will be exactly the same or even worse because you have missed the opportunity of making dramatic, positive change with your top three. Look to outsource these tasks: delegate them; ask a friend to help get them done; automate them or even pay someone to handle them because – and this is the magic bit – the items in your bottom three will be in someone else's top three!

As for the middle four, you'll always get these done somehow. Hidden within them may even be your potential... a new, currently unrefined skill or interest. Observe others, explore new learning and utilize the time you are saving from your no-longer-draining bottom three.

Spend time and resources learning and training on your top three or middle four, NOT your bottom three. It is unlikely you will ever enjoy those less compelling tasks, no matter how much more efficiently you attack them.

Refined 3-4-3 Simple Note:

Let's spend a moment on the Art of Successful Delegating.

You know you need to delegate and haven't yet cracked how to make it work for yourself or your delegated helper. The 3-4-3 strategy is made for you.

It is highly likely that up until now, whenever you need to free up time, the tasks you would delegate come from your top three or middle four, simply because you cannot believe anyone else would want to do your 'dirty laundry'.

And of course your helper can never complete those top three tasks to your quality standard and expectations or with the essence and spice that you would give, so you spend your time looking over their shoulder, micro-managing. Inevitably, you end up taking the damn thing back!

But there, deep in your bottom three, are tasks that you feel nothing for, which someone else (if you choose them correctly) will do better, faster and with less pain, because it falls within your delegate's top or middle categories.

Across a team you will be surprised how the 3-4-3s differ, creating an ideal opportunity to shift activities to the best exponent.

You get the gist: become aware and make your move!

41. FOCUS ON ONE

"The secret of getting ahead is getting started. The secret of getting started is breaking your complex overwhelming tasks into manageable tasks, and then starting on the first one."

Mark Twain (1835-1910)

I have noticed consistently that there can be just one action which, when committed to, produces certain new results. But more often than not that task gets lost in a list of sometimes overwhelming actions that slow progress, increase doubt and prompt resistance and boredom at the lack of progress.

So what is the answer?

Well, you may be bombarded with meetings, events, options, information and challenges, each of these grasping at your concentration and focus. It is tough work to make personal change stick.

My research concurs with that of many schools and institutions that have studied willpower. It is strongest when focused, like a laser, on *one* thing.

At the beginning of a particular year I carried three 'resolutions' and experienced the challenge of multiple demands on my willpower. I then made the decision to choose just one item and pointed all my willpower at that challenge. In making this choice the challenge or resolution stayed in focus and my goal was achieved within the month.

As the following month began, I could then chose a new single focus, and, in turn, nothing became more important than that.

I challenge you to audit your must-do, need-to, and have-to lists and home in on one thing (for this week or this month) and do it.

You will strengthen your ability to focus on any one thing and you'll experience more and more developmental and transformational change. It is a skill that you will enhance each time you put it to use. You will develop a powerful new single-item achievement muscle.

So make it just one thing and you will succeed.

42. PUT YOUR FACE BACK WHILE IT'S STILL WARM

*"Experience is not what happens to you;
it's what you do with what happens to you."*

Aldous Huxley (1894-1963)

One of my favourite phrases from the late Wayne Dyer, prolific author and speaker, is: "If you change the way you look at things, the things you look at change." In essence, your attitude at any moment predetermines how you experience everything that's going on in that moment.

Your reality (how it feels to be you, with all your pressures, joys, successes and tensions) obviously feels absolutely real. And without giving it any conscious thought, it seems to be what it is – real, no options. It just is.

The way you hold your reality (your mindset) sets up your behaviour: what you cause and what you experience from that moment on.

The truth is, your situation is possibly quite different from what you're telling yourself. Which bits of it are you noticing and focusing on the most, perhaps habitually?

To change your reality (and you can) you need to be ready to defy it! Let me illustrate.

Over a three-week period some time ago I found I was carrying an attitude of, 'I've got loads to do and too little time.' It was leavened with a bit of 'I don't know where to start', with a dash of 'I'm not actually getting anywhere' thrown in. This was a potent mix that left me feeling tense and at times anxious and irritable (reacting impatiently with loved ones). I wore this attitude physically, in the form of facial expressions. Close friends would often tell me to 'put your face back while it's still warm', as my grimace remained in place for too long.

During this period I also was carrying an unhelpful attitude, one of 'I never have time to focus'.

Put these together and the 'reality' at home and work had become tense, frantic and rushed. I was achieving, perhaps, but it didn't always feel like fun along the way.

You can always find a moment to view Facebook, Twitter, turn on the TV, read something irrelevant – anything that disproves a negative mindset. So here's a suggestion, which shifts attitudes and alters how you can experience your days:

A reality check.

Explore a way to defy your current reality, to the extent that you barely still believe in it. You may not be able to convince yourself of the absolute opposite mindset – 'I have abundant time to achieve everything today' – but you might be able to get closer to more positive thoughts, like: 'I have time', 'I get things done', 'I find time'.

Find three examples of how the alternate reality is already true. Work hard at this; your mind will initially resist. If it's 'I will find time' you are working on, notice the gaps between meetings, the choices you have over the next ten minutes, etc.

When feelings and thoughts of the old mindset creep back in, consciously and deliberately shift your thinking to the reality you actually want, and that feels better.

It will not take long to work this through and very soon your new, desired, shifted reality will become the norm.

43. SOME LIGHT WEEDING

*"Don't judge each day by the harvest you reap,
but by the seeds that you plant."*

Robert Louis Stevenson (1850-1894)

I am blessed with a great garden, but would not describe myself as a gardener, or as being especially motivated to get to work on a flower bed. However, walking around the garden in the sun one morning a weeding metaphor came to mind.

Looking around I could see that the weeds, although not yet dominant, were many and thriving. Within a few weeks they would undoubtedly dominate the flowerbeds and prevent the desired plants from flourishing. It didn't seem urgent to attend to the weeds just yet, but, once done, the space for growth would expand and create the opportunity to add new plants. In both cases this minimizes the opportunity for weeds to return.

Do you get the metaphor? Your mind, desk, plans, shelves, diaries, cupboards and wardrobes all attract weeds. They seem unimportant and inoffensive until you reach the point where concentration suffers, focus is hindered, you tire quickly and you lose sight of your goal. Progress has slowed without you noticing and the dream gets lost. It's just as when a flowerbed becomes overburdened by untouched weeds, hiding or even harming the beautiful plants below.

Even if it is not yet spring, it is always a good time to weed out the unwanted, create some space to allow the good stuff to grow, and plant new ideas and initiatives.

My challenge to you is to schedule 30 minutes this week to:

1. Scan and weed your desk, your diary, your involvement in peripheral projects. Spot them, decide on them, and remove them.

2. Become mindful of and reduce your watching, reading or listening to negative news; avoid negative people.

3. Fill any obvious gaps with exposure to positive and inspiring people, places or events.

As you get into the regular habit of weeding, turn to your newly streamlined cupboards, email inbox, garden sheds, bookshelves and allow your magnificence to blossom!

44. CONTROL-ALT-DELETE

"We cannot change anything until we accept it."

Carl Jung (1875-1961)

One of the first actions I take when my PC becomes irritatingly slow is 'Control–Alt–Delete'. This rudimentary step displays the processes running and the amount of the computer's memory taken up working on each. The absence of further useful knowledge means that I rarely do anything with this information, but remain curious about what the processes are. Are they important, are they good for me, does my PC need to be running them at all?

Just like my cluttered PC, your list can be incredibly long. Every item uses some of your power/focus/RAM. Every loose piece of paper on your desk, notes around the home, calls yet to be returned, active tasks, dormant tasks, old mistakes, new ideas, plans, dreams or doubts – all use up part of your processing power.

Your brilliant capacity means that much of this goes unnoticed and you go about your day comfortably, largely unperturbed. As the list grows beyond normal and acceptable levels, your capacity to be at your best and energy to work on new challenges can become exhausted.

My challenge for you in this *Simple Note* is to press your personal Control–Alt–Delete. Grab a pen and paper and make the list. Stay with the list and go beyond the obvious. What are you running/carrying/holding in your mind?

Return to your list over the course of a few days as you become conscious of new 'processes'.

Now review your list. There may be obvious items that use up the majority of your memory power, and necessarily so, and that tends to be where we apply our focus.

Next, notice the long, long list of seemingly insignificant things that when combined are taking up space in your capacity and using up yet more energy. This list requires an immediate purge.

What can you complete, let go of, consciously 'press-pause', or otherwise address right now?

Make these decisions and you WILL notice the difference.

Consider incorporating 'Control–Alt–Delete' make your personal maintenance programme monthly or more ofetn if the list seems long or you frequently experience a memory-is-full emotion.

45. THE MOST IMPORTANT MEETING

"You are today where your thoughts have brought you; you will be tomorrow where your thoughts take you."

James Allen (1864-1912)

A quick view of your calendar for the upcoming week will undoubtedly reveal days full of meetings, back-to-back on some occasions, with no thinking or breathing space in between.

The culture in many companies with which I work seems to dictate and perpetuate the meeting habit. Meetings are invaluable, some of the time, in achieving progress on an objective or two. However,

I have observed their ability to consume teams, divisions and even entire companies. Far too many people are involved in each of them and the agendas and action lists inevitably grow out of control. And that's a recipe for reduced effectiveness.

But one particular type of meeting, potentially the most valuable to you and your journey, tends to get scant attention.

My challenge in this *Simple Note* is that you immediately schedule the **most important meeting**. It is simply a meeting with yourself. The 'you-on-you' meeting can be strategic or tactical, reflective or active, and have similar intent to the plethora of meetings you would otherwise attend each day.

You may convince yourself that you have meetings with yourself already as you snatch a moment to contemplate a project, an intention or an initiative. But until they are formally included in your schedule they're usually sub-optimal! They only occur as you walk between other meetings, to the car park or the train, on the journey itself. They're wedged into the gaps with no agenda or specific focus, random thoughts, open to every possible distraction, and almost always in utterly inappropriate environments.

Would you seriously allow your team or project meetings to take place like that? If you did, what result would you expect from them?

If you want to shift your thinking, your performance and your results, then adopt a 'you-on-you' communication plan. Your meeting need not necessarily be in a conference room with a set of charts; simply set it up in a way that will work best. Conduct this internal conversation in a quiet place, for as long as you can handle being with the single participant (start with ten minutes). And don't complicate it; just have one or two agenda items/thoughts to focus on (and you won't be surprised to hear that I recommend just one).

Ten minutes a day? An hour a week? You could even invite expert guests to join you. Create some frequency, perhaps even make notes (just as Einstein did as he spent time working on his thinking). Just stop putting off this incredibly valuable investment of your time.

Experiment with your Most Important Meeting. Vary the structure until you find what works best for you. Range from no structure – a quiet meditative moment simply reflecting on where you are and what's going on for you right now – to a structured agenda to focus your thinking. Your agenda may include some or all of these questions:

What has been my greatest success since my last meeting?

What is the greatest challenge I face right now?

What support would make everything flow more easily? (Don't restrict your answers; create your perfect wish list.)

What resources do I have right now?

What missing or insufficient resources do I need?

What am I attracting?

What do I want – what do I really want?

What could I stop doing, or start doing, and what do I need to continue to keep doing?

But most of all... *Keep It Simple.*

Just do it.

46. YOU'RE HERE, NOW, NOWHERE ELSE - ACT LIKE IT

"Our self-image and our habits tend to go together.
Change one and you will automatically change the other."

Dr Maxwell Maltz (1889-1975)

One of my coaches, Drew Rozell, provided much inspiration to me during our work together and through the articles that he's penned. He asserted this *Simple Note's* title, "You're Here, Now, Nowhere Else – Act Like It", a few years ago in one of his newsletters. I still carry it with me and recite it often.

Have you been in situations or places where you would rather be somewhere else? Were your thoughts and attention elsewhere?

Have you been at an event, meeting or in a situation that simply wasn't pushing your buttons, but it was not appropriate for you just to walk away?

In such situations, you have become a person of two minds. You're less than fully effective, your concentration is impaired, your creativity is hindered, your mood shifts (in the wrong direction), you are not fully present and you're probably less fun to be with. It is simply not a good place.

Over the next few days try to realize that you are here now, nowhere else... so act like it, in all circumstances in which you find yourself. Does your mind wander? Do you feel fidgety or irritable?

Here are five thought-starters to shift you quickly to the more powerful single-minded place:

1. If I absolutely loved this situation what would I be doing, saying; how would I be standing, talking, contributing? Whatever your answer, do it.

2. What have I not yet noticed about the situation, people, objects, sounds, attitudes, moods?

3. What might be my role here, assuming I haven't fully realized it yet?

4. If there is something for me to learn here, what might it be?

5. If there is something for me to teach or share here, what might it be?

Carry these questions, or some of your own design, into the next week's meetings. As soon as you catch yourself mentally drifting out of the room or off the conference call, pose a question, answer it and act on your responses.

Enjoy, be fully present and thrive with your single mind centred in the place you find yourself.

47. THE FIVE PEOPLE WHO INFLUENCE YOU MOST

*"If you always live with those who are lame,
you will yourself learn to limp."*

Latin Proverb

The five people with whom you spend most time have the greatest impact on your:

1.   Mood.

2.   Attitude.

3.   Current thinking and view of the world.

4.   Range of default decisions.

5.   Vision and hope for the future.

Consciously or unconsciously, this select group of people is shaping your thinking, sharing their ideas and views and providing the space for you to share yours.

If there is something about your mood or attitude or current situation that isn't quite right, or is in some way off track, then look again at your High-Influence Five. Are they actually serving you, your goals and your desires? Do they stretch, support, challenge? Are they even remotely interested in your personal growth, your passions and dreams?

Who are the people you have spent the most time with over the course of the last few weeks? Who are these people you surround yourself with in the office, in meetings, in social situations?

Once you have identified the five most important people, consider what is going on in their world. What is their focus, are they on the way up or down? Are they hopeful, inspiring? Are they stuck or making progress? Are they a mix of these or all of a type?

How your current High-Influence Five came together is often a result of your recent history or your geographical location. Until this group is configured by conscious design, your ability to shift your mood, attitude and results will be difficult. Remember, each time you return to the five, you reset back to the level of the five.

Of your current panel, are there any you should reduce your exposure to? Who could join? Who will support you and gear you up for greater things?

Take action this week. The action necessary to make a change may be major, in which case *start now*. You could even begin interviewing potential candidates to join your team.

48. THE PURPOSEFUL TEAM

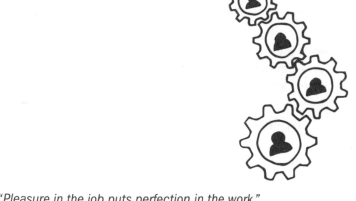

"Pleasure in the job puts perfection in the work."

Aristotle (384-322 BC)

Many teams find themselves just existing, delivering the stream of actions that are required and occasionally a few more.

Among you and your team, there will invariably be a nagging sense that more is possible. I am sure you have often heard the 1+1=3 synergy story, the sum of the parts is more powerful than any of the individual elements. Indeed significant greater potential almost always lies within reach for your team.

Consider the following line of enquiry for your team, and allow the answers to guide your way ahead.

1. What do I personally want or get from being part of a team?

Responses from the group will be different. Bringing them to the surface helps each team member realize that together they can achieve their desires. And they are not all in it for the same thing.

2. Who are our customers?

More than just those who buy your products and services, this group also includes stakeholders, contributors, suppliers – everyone with whom your team impacts upon.

3. What do they say about us?

You could even ask them, although they may already be communicating messages to you in various verbal and non-verbal ways.

4. What do we want them to say about us?

Be as adventurous and as outrageous as you wish and stretch beyond what seems possible from where you are.

5. What stops you?

Design the Change. This means identifying and clearing out the barriers to progress. Start with the easy changes and build belief and momentum from there.

This should be the unconscious strategy for all successful teams. Having the conversation and bringing what's really going on to the surface – making it conscious – will inspire the change journey for your team.

49. THINKER THINKS, PROVER PROVES

"What we think, we become."

Gautama Siddhartha (Sixth-Century B.C)

Any hypothesis or assumption you are holding tends to influence how you set yourself up to experience the day – what you are aware of, and what you choose to see, hear, feel and notice.

You may often not even be aware of what your active assumptions are, since they have been formed over years without you realizing it. They become ingrained quite deeply, as a product of:

1.   Your parenting.

2.   Your environments (home, school, work).

3. Your friends.

4. What you read, watch and consume.

5. Who you spend most of your time with.

Your assumptions are playing out in all areas of your life and they dictate the sense of comfort, the success and the joy you derive from:

1. Relationships.

2. Work, your job role and the success you achieve.

3. Health and wellbeing.

4. Finances.

At some level of consciousness, you are thinking and embedding these assumptions. The rest of your brain is at work scouring and scanning your world to prove them to be true. Your sensory tool kit is off finding evidence to confirm the hypothesis. *The Thinker thinks, the Prover proves.*

Where you find exceptions counter to your assumptions, whether you welcome or detest them, you tag them as rare and incorrectly aligned phenomena. You 'in effect' reject them as non-admissible evidence.

As an example, a long-time client of mine was experienced ongoing career success, but always coupled with work overload, physical demands and time pressures that affected her entire life.

In dialogue we discovered that deep in the background was her assumption that she would always struggle in senior roles and, that with greater responsibility came greater struggle. While not attempting to delude her into believing that senior roles do not bring new and stretching challenges, the extent to which it was weighing on her did not necessarily have to be a given. It was clear that her 'unconscious' assumption was true.

So we experimented with new hypotheses, ones that her mind might just be able to accept may be true. In senior roles, opportunities to change ways or working frequently present themselves. A productive yet peaceful existence as possible! And slowly my client began to embrace a liberating new hypothesis. Resistance and doubt surfaced, but the assumptions at work were challenged and changed.

My challenge to you this week is to consider what assumptions you are holding in four key areas of your life: relationships, health, finances, work success. Then take a look at your current and recurring results; they will be an almost direct match to the assumptions you make.

Could you upgrade one of them?

Your brilliant brain can go about achieving whatever you task it to do. Think it, and make it so. Choose something nice!

50. JUDGING ME

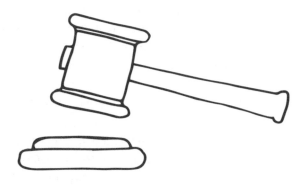

"Trust yourself. You know more than you think you do."

Benjamin Spock (1903-1998)

While in conversation with a coaching client, we noticed how often she was judging herself and the situations in which she found herself. She was unconsciously judging whether they were good enough or whether she was good enough. She insisted on comparing herself to some unconscious, unspecified, virtually impossible-to-attain criteria. The speed with which these self-judgments kicked in instantly affected her attitude and mood, and altered the words, tone of voice and general satisfaction she allowed herself to experience.

When the judge runs out of control, absolutely nothing seems good enough.

Do you have an inner-judge that jumps in and provokes the same? This is not helpful, other than to help identify potential areas of personal development. But this is false logic. For most of us it lays out some imagined, ridiculously perfect world or version of yourself that is delusional and simply makes it easy to beat yourself up or set yourself up for disappointment.

Stop judging. It hurts, and the bad feelings it engenders only compound over time.

I challenge you to go one week without judging anything or anyone, most of all yourself.

An alternate course of action is to notice your inner-judge pontificating. Perhaps make a note of the judgement in your notebook, laugh at it, then discard it. Accept yourself, and the situations that show up, as if they were great... even if they don't appear to be.

One week with no judging is good – relish it, it's okay. These situations don't have to be anything else; they don't need to be better or worse, faster or slower. They are simply what they are.

Go on, try it for just one week. It will be enough to remove the judge from the bench.

During your week there is a chance you will experience one or more of the following:

- The judge screaming to be heard. Pull the metaphorical wig over her or his face.

- People noticing you acting differently and asking if you're okay!

- Things feeling 'lighter' and not as disastrous as those around you may suggest.

- Your ego panicking that you are missing out on something (not true) or deluding yourself.

- The euphoric feeling of 'everything is okay'!

Good luck and as always keep it simple.

KEEP IT SIMPLE

Well, congratulations! You've reached the end of this collection of *Simple Notes*. Taken one-a-week, you may find yourself exploring a year's worth of personal evolution ideas. I hope you have found a number of *Simple Notes* to support your journey, shift your thinking and challenge you to change.

The late Stephen Covey stated very specifically in his work (most notably *The Seven Habits of Highly Effective People*) that to really embed new information, go and teach it to someone else within a few days. This paradigm shift (from learner to teacher) helps the brain connect with information in different ways, often helping you 'get it' even more deeply than when you were simply a learner.

So why not go and teach this stuff? All I ask is that you mention this book, and my work, and if it helps others then they can find their way to me and a store of even more *Simple Notes*. Teach them, discuss these tried-and-true tips, and work on them alone, or with a partner or a team. A number of people have told me that when they have worked through one or more of the *Simple Notes*, you will invariably find that ideas emerge and the ensuing solutions are even better.

SOURCES OF INSPIRATION

Dr. Wayne W. Dyer

The late Wayne Dyer is perhaps my most absolute source of inspiration. His work is normally the first place I turn to for thoughts, ideas and what to do next. He has authored more than 30 books and created many audio programmes and videos that have changed my thinking and helped spawn ideas of my own that show up in my *Simple Notes* so many times. His books include *Manifest Your Destiny*, *Wisdom of the Ages*, *There's a Spiritual Solution to Every Problem*, and the *New York Times* bestsellers *10 Secrets for Success and Inner Peace*, *The Power of Intention*, *Change Your Thoughts – Change Your Life*, and *Excuses Begone*! Which have all been featured as national public television specials in the USA. www.drwaynedyer.com

Thomas Leonard

To me Thomas was a founding father of modern coaching, a prolific creator of content and a remarkable coach who I had the honour of working with in two live events in London before his death in 2003. He founded Coach University in 1992, the International Coaching Federation in 1994, authored literally hundreds of coaching development classes and programmes and launched Coachville in 2000, which became my main source of learning and development. www.coachville.com, www.thomasleonard.com.

Kate Duffy

I have known Kate since we were participants in a coaching programme ('Simply Effective' with Jay Perry and Scott Wintrip) in 2001. Since then we have coached each other, worked on client coaching projects and with Joanne Dunleavy delivered the *Attitude Vitamin*, a series of 15-minute inspirational ideas to shift your attitude at the beginning of the day.

Kate Duffy is a Certified Life Coach with a natural results orientation. Kate's background includes Non-Profit Leadership, Sales, Management Coaching and HR Business Partner. Her current passion and focus is recovery and life coaching; with those struggling from addiction and for those in recovery who want to build a phenomenal life. www.kateduffy.com.

Michael Neill

I have been reading Michael's work since 2002 as a subscriber to his blog and cannot recall a single article that has not been valuable to me. Michael Neill is an internationally renowned transformative coach and the best-selling author of five books, including *The Inside-Out Revolution* and *The Space Within*. His weekly radio show, *Living from the Inside Out*, has been a listener favourite on Hay House Radio for more than a decade. www.michaelneill.org

Drew Rozell

As an avid reader of the 'Drewsletter' since 2003, Drew has always influenced my thinking. In 2009 I engaged him as my coach and worked with him for a year, one in which I acquired a new business and took significant changes in the direction of my own coaching business. Drew holds a PhD in Social Psychology, and is a writer and personal coach who works with clients to raise their level of awareness and live more attractive lives. His work is now focused on living a very cool life, with a book and development programme to boot. www.verycoollife.com, www.drewrozell.com

Recommendations to follow:

Instagram:
simontyler_official (me!)
deepakchopra
eckharttolle manifestation_manifesto

Twitter:
@simplysimont (me!)
@simonsinek
@thesecret
@BreneBrown
@TheGoldenMirror

Other sources of Keep It Simple inspiration:

The Artist's Way – Julia Cameron
Reed Business Information Inc. – ISBN: 978-0330343589

The Seven Spiritual Laws of Success – Deepak Chopra
Reed Business Information Inc. – ISBN: 978-1878424112

The Power of Now – Eckhart Tolle
Namaste Publishing – ISBN: 978-1577314806

The Four Agreements – Don Miguel Ruiz
Amber Allen Publishing – ISBN: 978-1878424310

The Moses Code – James F Twyman
Hay House Inc. – ISBN: 978-1401917883

The Slight Edge – Jeff Olson
Greenleaf Book Group Press - ISBN: 978-1626340466

ABOUT THE AUTHOR

After years of countering it, Simon Tyler eventually and wisely accepted his childhood taunt, 'Simple Simon,' and brought simplicity to his coaching practice, his speaking and his clients' businesses.

As one of the world's leading business coaches and motivational speakers, Simon has enabled scores of business executives, leaders, owners and solopreneurs to become increasingly successful by exploring their own intellect and applying a range of innovative and personally enabling techniques.

Simon is a renowned motivational speaker, much respected for his ability to deliver refreshingly honest, acutely insightful and eminently practical talks to large audiences that challenge consensus thinking, break through barriers and redefine connections through the power of simplicity, attitude and personal impact.

Simon coaches executives and teams and speaks at team meetings, seminars and conferences. His talks are guaranteed to inspire, motivate and, most importantly, deliver results. Using humour and audience interaction and real life stories, his style is light, lively, memorable and entertaining, but also pragmatic – full of easy-to-apply techniques and tools for each member of his audience to put to immediate use for themselves and their teams. Just like these *Simple Notes*.

He takes on a limited number of clients each year so he can dedicate himself to their personal transformation. For speaking enquiries and to find out more, visit his website www.simontyler.com and subscribe to receive the latest *Simple Notes.*

The *Simple Notes* have grown out of Simon's belief that "Keeping It Simple" is the best way.

He can be contacted via his website www.simontyler.com.

Contact the author for coaching, mentoring, facilitating and speaking

contact@simontyler.com
www.simontyler.com
LinkedIn - http://uk.linkedin.com/in/simontyler/
Twitter - @simplysimont
Instagram - simontyler_official

Also by the author
The Impact Code – published by LID Publishing
Simple Notes – published on the web every two weeks, free subscription at simontyler.com.

FOR OTHER TITLES IN THE SERIES...

CONCISE ADVICE LAB

SMALL BOOKS: BIG IDEAS

CLEVER CONTENT, DYNAMIC IDEAS, PRACTICAL
SOLUTIONS AND ENGAGING VISUALS –
A CATALYST TO INSPIRE NEW WAYS OF THINKING
AND PROBLEM-SOLVING IN A COMPLEX WORLD

conciseadvicelab.com